the pit bull life

the pit bull life

A DOG LOVER'S COMPANION

Deirdre Franklin and Linda Lombardi

The Countryman Press

A division of W. W. Norton & Company

Independent Publishers Since 1923

For information about permission to reproduce selections from this book,
write to Permissions, The Countryman Press,
500 Fifth Avenue, New York, NY 10110

For information about special discounts for bulk purchases, please contact
W. W. Norton Special Sales at specialsales@wwnorton.com or 800-233-4830

Manufacturing by RR Donnelley, Shenzhen
Book design by Chris Welch
Production manager: Devon Zahn

Library of Congress Cataloging-in-Publication Data

Names: Franklin, Deirdre, author. | Lombardi, Linda, 1961– , author.
Title: The pit bull life : a dog lover's companion / Deirdre Franklin and
   Linda Lombardi.
Description: New York, NY : The Countryman Press, 2016. | Includes
   bibliographical references and index.
Identifiers: LCCN 2016030019 | ISBN 9781581573626 (hardcover)
Subjects: LCSH: Pit bull terriers.
Classification: LCC SF429.P58 F733 2016 | DDC 636.755/9—dc23 LC record
available at lccn.loc.gov/2016030019

The Countryman Press
www.countrymanpress.com

A division of W. W. Norton & Company
500 Fifth Avenue, New York, NY 10110
www.wwnorton.com

10 9 8 7 6 5 4 3 2 1

THIS BOOK IS DEDICATED TO
THE MILLIONS OF PEOPLE
WHO HAVE OPENED THEIR HEARTS
AND HOMES TO THESE RESILIENT AND
OFTEN MISUNDERSTOOD DOGS.
IN LOVING MEMORY OF EMILY UGARENKO.

contents

picture a pit bull

When you hear the word *dog*, what's the first image that comes to mind? Once upon a time in America, chances are it would have looked like a pit bull.

To all kinds of storytellers in the early twentieth century, the pit bull was the obvious choice to represent every boy's best friend. Maybe the most famous example is Pete the Pup from *The Little Rascals*, the dog with that funny black circle around his eye who's still recognized today. Petey was in fact doubly a pit bull: He was registered as both an American pit bull terrier and a Staffordshire terrier, two of the purebreds that fall in the pit bull category. Also still familiar is Buster Brown and his dog Tige, characters from a comic strip that started in 1902. They're most famous for a licensing deal that outlasted both the strip and its creator, convincing moms to buy Buster Brown-brand shoes for their children for many decades.

Another canine advertising icon with a long career was RCA's Nipper, the familiar black and white pup listening curiously to a recording of his master's voice. While some call Nipper a pit bull, no one knows the breed of the real dog he was based on. But as you'll see as you read this book, his unknown heritage makes him fit in all the more.

Real-life pit bulls were also the companions of some famous humans early in the last century. John Steinbeck's better-known canine is the standard poodle that accompanied him across the country in *Travels with Charley*, but he also once had a pit bull named Jiggs. President Teddy Roosevelt owned a pit bull called Pete, although—as a car-chaser, escape artist, and biter of ambassadors and senators—Pete was not the good role model for the nation's dogs that you might want to see in that august position. Reporters enjoyed joking that part of Pete's job was to defend the president from reporters.

On a more heartwarming note, Helen Keller wrote in her autobiography that she had "many dog friends," including "honest, homely bull terriers." You'll sometimes read her Phiz described as a Boston bulldog or Boston terrier, but don't be confused—those were two of the names pit bulls went by early in the century. As we'll see later, not only have pit bulls gone by many different names, but many dogs of unknown ancestry have gone

by the name of pit bulls. Many still do, and it's unmistakable from a photo that they can claim Phiz as one of their own.

The Pit Bull Hall of Fame

Pit bulls had roles in significant moments in history, too, and some became celebrities in their own right. One, Bud, was the forefather of all dogs who love to go for a ride in the car. Dr. Horatio Nelson Jackson and Sewall K. Crocker set out on the first transcontinental trip by automobile from Sacramento in 1903, at a time when there were no gas stations or road maps and only about 150 miles of paved road in the whole country. Jackson apparently thought he had everything he needed for the trip except a canine companion, and solved that problem in Idaho when a man sold him Bud for $15. Bud got the same sort of breathless newspaper coverage that we'd see on the animal-obsessed internet today.

Pit bulls were also often our comrades in war. A dog named Sallie was honored for her service to the 11th Pennsylvania Infantry during the Civil War; a statue to her memory (photo opposite) still stands in Gettysburg today. The brindle bully Sgt. Stubby was treated as a true war hero for his service in World War I. He met presidents, rode in parades of veterans, rated an obituary in the *New York Times*, and was even stuffed and preserved at the Smithsonian.

In Stubby's obituary, we see the qualities that pit bulls were admired for through the decades. "He seemed to know that the

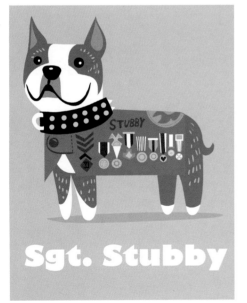
Sgt. Stubby

greatest service he could render was comfort and cheerfulness," the author wrote. But that wasn't the only skill he offered:

> Hearing a sound in the stillness of the night, the dog, who guarded sleeplessly, stole out of the trenches and recognized a German. Attempts by the German to deceive the dog were futile. Seizing his prisoner by the breeches, Stubby held on until help arrived.

Stubby was reportedly a hero even when off duty—one time when he was granted leave in Paris, a little girl stopped in a public square to pat him on the head:

> The girl started to leave the square; Stubby pulled her back from the path of a runaway horse.

THE AMERICAN WATCH-DOG

The pit bull was so fundamentally American that more than one wartime artist used this dog to represent the nation. The image told the world that Americans were like Stubby: cheerful and friendly, but strong and determined, and would rise to the occasion when bravery was called for.

How Times Have Changed

This history may be surprising, because for many people today the pit bull is the farthest thing possible from a charming mascot for children's shoes. Keep your ears and eyes open in any kind of popular culture and you'll find references like this one:

> Trying a brand-new menu item at McDonald's isn't risky. You know what's risky? Petting a stray pit bull.
>
> —McDonald's radio ad

It's clear that in our culture today, *pit bull* has become shorthand for something very different from a friend to little boys and brave comrade to the troops.

How did the image of these dogs change so much? The short answer is basically, "It's complicated." The long answer, we'll look at a bit more in Chapter 2. But however it happened, Pete the Pup would have a very different life today. Sure, much has gotten better for dogs in general over the past century—from the laws protecting animals to the advanced veterinary care to all the fancy toys and treats you can buy. He'd have a much higher standard of living. But he and his humans would face some unique issues at the same time.

What This Means for You

It takes a loyal, caring, and devoted person to love any dog, but it takes a little bit more than that to own a dog known as a pit bull. This is not because pit bulls are inherently different, but because you might face challenges that most dog owners do not even know exist, such as breed bans. (Although most pit bull owners would say that they *are* different—especially when it comes to stealing bedsheets and snuggling with all of their heart.) If this were a book about golden retrievers, we could simply write about how to train your dog, brush his coat, and maybe some common health issues. It's unfortunate that a book about pit bulls needs to be more than that. Because of their special legal situation and reputation today, if you live with a pit bull, you need to be more than a good friend and caretaker—you need to be a well-informed advocate. But it's worth it, because we know that keeping a pit bull as a companion animal is worth its weight in gold-plated dog biscuits.

In this book, we'll present many kinds of information that will help you negotiate tricky situations in which you may find yourself. Whether you're simply educating a worried neighbor or fighting to protect your dog from a breed-specific law, you need to start with a strong foundation of facts.

We don't expect this book to be the last word on anything. Research on dog behavior, long thought uninteresting, has exploded in recent years and continues going strong; laws are changing, often for the better, as we write. But we hope to give you much to think about and provide the resources to help your best friend.

what is a pit bull?

What is a pit bull? Sounds like a simple question. It's a breed of dog, right?

True, one part of the answer is easy: why "bull" is in the name. *Bulldog* and various similar names are used for types of dogs bred to work with large game and large livestock, such as bulls. Today's familiar squat English bulldog is no longer suited to that job, but its ancestors were leggier and much less compact—in fact, if you saw one in a nineteenth-century painting, you'd probably call it a pit bull.

But beyond that, what counts as a pit bull is more complicated than you probably think. Nowadays we think of a breed as a dog that looks a certain way and is granted official status by a national kennel club. But it hasn't always been that simple, and it sure isn't that simple now for the dogs called pit bulls.

In fact, several similar breeds with similar names have been recognized and renamed over the course of the twentieth century—and it turns out that's the most straightforward part of it. As we'll see in this chapter, the term is used for many dogs that on closer examination aren't members of those breeds at all. Put that together with the stereotypes and our confusion about the connection between breed and behavior, and it spells trouble for pit bull-type dogs.

Bully Cousins

To start, there is actually no officially recognized purebred dog called pit bull or pit bull terrier. The term *pit bull* is best understood as describing a type of dog, like the term *retriever* or *hound*, and not a specific breed.

However, there are at least three breeds with some kind of official kennel club recognition that someone is likely to mean if they say they have a "purebred pit bull." Two of these are registered by the well-known American Kennel Club: the American Staffordshire terrier and the Staffordshire bull terrier. Another is the American pit bull terrier, registered and originally recognized by the United Kennel Club (UKC).

As with many other sets of similar purebreds, the differences among these breeds are of intense importance to fanciers but can be rather obscure to the average dog lover. We'll do our best to give a simple version of the somewhat confusing history and relationships.

A Pit Bull by Any Other Name

The American pit bull terrier is the oldest recognized breed of the three. The UKC was founded in 1898, and the first breed in its registry was given the official name "American (pit) bull terrier"—(official parentheses included!).

What many people don't realize, though, is that dog registry organizations don't invent or develop breeds—they just invite breeds that already exist to become part of their club. Diane Jessup, an expert on the American pit bull terrier (APBT), says that she can trace the ancestry of her dogs back to the 1870s, and it existed as a type long before that. So that first kennel club recognition and registration is merely a moment in a long history of these dogs.

Matters then got more complicated in the 1930s, when some of the people with APBTs registered by the UKC decided they wanted their dogs to be recognized by the AKC, too, and lobbied to be included. The AKC gave the breed a different name, Staffordshire terrier, for reasons that no doubt had more to do with people and dog club politics than actual dogs. As dog club skeptics ourselves, the explanation we like best for why they chose this name comes from the late author and animal trainer Vicki Hearne:

> Staffordshire is in England, and this is an American dog, but it sounds better to say "Staffordshire," so people did.

That specific name didn't actually last long, but the "Staffordshire" part of it really took off—the AKC liked it so much they used it twice. Later, they decided to recognize another breed called the Staffordshire bull terrier. At that point, it renamed the Staffordshire terrier as the American Staffordshire terrier.

Got it? And this is all leaving aside the fact that there's also another AKC breed called the bull terrier—that's the egg-headed dog that's often all white, that you might remember as the mascot for Target stores.

Probably the most interesting part of all this is the fact that originally the American pit bull terrier and what's now the American Staffordshire terrier (AmStaff) were the same dogs. The two kennel clubs had different goals, though, so they began to breed in different ways. Dogfighting was still accepted by the UKC at the time—the club only took a position against it later—so for that association, temperament and working ability were considered paramount. The AKC focused on what's called conformation—how the dog looks. "They bred them to be show dogs and pet dogs, bigger and heavier and prettier," says Jessup. Even then, there was still some back and forth between the registries throughout the twentieth century, each letting in the other's dogs at various points.

And to end on one more note of confusion: Although all these dogs have "terrier" in the name, terriers are a type that is bred for a very different job—digging into the ground to catch small game, then shaking and killing it. The original job of the pit bull type was to grab large game and hold it for the hunters. Later, pit bulls were used for tasks such as holding a cattle still for branding while specifically *not* killing it.

What's in a Name?

If the history of the officially recognized breeds that are commonly called pit bulls seems a bit bewildering, hang onto your hat, because now we're getting to the really confusing part. It turns out that most of the dogs we call pit bulls today are in fact none of the above.

"The basic thing people need to understand is that the American pit bull terrier today is actually a rare breed," says Jessup. The AmStaff and Staffordshire are fairly uncommon as well—Staffordshire is the seventy-seventh most common breed registered by the AKC in 2014 and AmStaff is number eighty-two.

So, how are urban animal shelters and rescues full of homeless pit bulls? It's because outside the specialized world of the kennel club, what defines a breed isn't registration papers.

What Is a Breed, Anyway?

What defines a dog breed has changed fundamentally in the last century or so. Kennel clubs and other organizations that decide what an "official" member of a breed is, are a fairly recent thing historically—the AKC was only founded in 1884. People had been giving names to certain types of dogs for centuries before that, and none of them had registration papers to rely on

So how did anyone know what breed a dog was before that? Basically, in the old days, breed identification came down to the old "If it looks like a duck and quacks like a duck . . ." No one asks to see a duck's registration papers, but we have no trouble recognizing those birds swimming on that pond over there.

So, if there were no registries keeping track of who was related to who, what did it even mean to be a breed in the first place? Biologists Raymond and Lorna Coppinger studied this question in their research with shepherds across Europe who still work in the traditional ways and have many different recognized types of livestock-guarding dogs with different names. What interested them is that these breeds are not the products of controlled, arranged matings. The shepherds have no system for separating out a female in heat, so the dogs choose who mates with who.

Without controlling breeding, how can dogs even develop into a breed? Human choice does come into play, but only later: Once you've got the puppies, you keep the ones that suit you and get rid of the rest. A dog that chases sheep is culled, a dog that doesn't stick with the flock gets lost and isn't part of the breeding population anymore . . . and so on. The ones that are left have the right behavioral tendencies to guard livestock.

Note that there's nothing in that explanation about how the dogs look, which is what we think is fundamental to the definition of a breed. The dogs do end up with fairly consistent appearance, but that's largely a side effect, not the goal. Maybe because they're working in cold places, big dogs with thicker coats are more successful. Maybe it's randomness—if no one in the first group of dogs carried the gene for a certain color, none of the descendants will be that color.

The Coppingers did find some effects of what you might call fashion in appearance. It would be surprising if they didn't, since this seems to be such an intrinsically human tendency. There are regional preferences for color, for example. But on the whole, dog breeds did not arise because humans took two dogs that looked a certain way, put them together to get more of the same, then kept track of it on a piece of paper. And yet no one had any trouble knowing what a breed was, as The Coppingers relate:

But how should a breed be identified? Years ago, I asked a shepherd in Portugal, "Is this an Estrela mountain dog?" and he replied, "Are these the Estrela mountains?" And, voilà, a new breed is born!

How Times Have Changed

How do we decide what is a pit bull? You could rewrite the conversation on the previous page, starring two people looking at a short-coated dog with a blocky head:

"Is this a pit bull?" "Are we in an urban animal shelter?" And voilà, a pit bull is born!

But there's a big difference in the story now: It's that we have a very different idea of what *breed* means. For the shepherds, it was mainly about behavior. For modern Americans, it's all about how a dog looks.

Our pet dogs are no longer the product of generations of selection for a certain job. Today most breeding places priority on looking like a duck; how the critter quacks is less important. Appearance is how we define a purebred today, and the result of this kind of breeding is that in most cases a breed's traditional functions are no longer particularly good predictors of how a dog will behave. This now mostly works out okay, though, since most people don't need a dog to do a job anymore. You get a corgi because you think its big ears are cute, not because you have livestock that needs to be moved from place to place.

When it comes to the dogs we call pit bulls, this lack of connection between appearance and behavior is all the more true,

because most of them aren't even purebreds. They're the product of a random assortments of dog genes that happened to come out looking a similar way, so any chance of predictability about their behavior flies out the window. Yet we define breed by looks—so we call them pit bulls—and then we think that tells us something about how they will act.

This is no big deal for some other breeds where, if you adopt something called a Lab mix from a shelter, you assume it will like to swim and chase balls. But this isn't true for dogs that look like pit bulls. It would almost be funny that a pit bull is whatever a landlord or insurance salesman says it is, except that because of the stereotypes about them, it can be a matter of life and death. And, as we'll see in the next section, even people way more experienced than your landlord are wrong more often than not about which dogs are genetically pit bulls.

Shelter Dog Breeds Are in the Eye of the Beholder

Here's something most people don't know about shelters and rescues: Despite those breed labels on their websites and kennel runs, they don't usually know the genetic background of the dogs in their care. Yes, there are cases where a purebred dog is surrendered directly by its owner who passes on its registration papers, but that's a tiny minority. Most breed identification

Aside from the Names and Politics, What Are the Purebreds Like?

Diane Jessup couldn't be more passionate about the purebred American pit bull terrier (APBT). This is exactly why she is quick to discourage most people from owning one. "Get one because you have some kind of dog sport, weight pulling, something like that that you want to do," she says. "They are a working breed, and like other working breeds, like the border collie and the Jack Russell, they do not make the best pets."

Obviously that depends on what you're looking for in a pet, but the APBT is a dog that needs a job, not one that will be content with short walks and hanging out on the couch. Descriptions for the other two breeds give the same impression: they use words like *tenacious*, *stubborn*, *curious*, *impulsive*, and sometimes *bull-headed*. And remember that these are written by the people who love these dogs! They breed them that way on purpose because they enjoy these qualities. So, if that doesn't sound like fun to you, if you're looking for less energy and intensity, best to choose another breed. The Staffordshire Bull Terrier Club of America website cautions:

> These dogs crave attention, companionship, and are tireless love sponges. This can annoy those who are used to a dog that amuses itself, is content to sit in its basket, prefers the companionship of another dog, or will settle for a quick occasional pat.

Another factor to keep in mind is that given their history as fighting dogs, they're not always mellow with their own kind. Individuals vary, of course. If you don't want multiple dogs or dream of going to the dog park, that quality might not put you off, but it's not uncommon for these breeds to be dog aggressive or selective about which other dogs they will get along with.

However, that same history actually makes them exceptionally good with people. It was important that a fighting dog not redirect its attack to its handler. And, says Jessup, their lifestyle outside the ring called for this quality as well. "A fighting dog was raised by one guy, he gave it to another guy, that guy gave it to someone else so he could condition it, and then someone else might even handle it in the ring. So the dogs had to be like, pretty much whoever was holding the leash was their owner. They are loyal in their own way, but they just like people."

This means that despite their tough appearance, these breeds may not make good guard dogs—they're just too ready to make friends. But they are tough, at least in the sense of not being fussy. "They are not a complainy, whiney breed," Jessup says of the APBT. "They take what you give them and they are happy."

in shelters is done by staff who look at a dog, maybe pull out a breed book, and say, "That looks like a cross between a pug and a husky." They sure don't do DNA analysis, because that costs money that they don't have.

The fact that the breed identification is a guess doesn't usually make much difference, because they're really just a sort of useful advertising. If the dog looks like a beagle and you call it a bea-

gle mix, then it's going to get the attention of people who think beagles are cute. Especially nowadays when a lot of people search online for a pet, categorizing a dog that way puts it in front of the people who are most likely to adopt it.

But when it comes to pit bulls, the same guessing game can have drastic consequences. So, it's important to be aware that even professionals are actually really terrible at it—for reasons that are actually no fault of their own, because it's a game that's impossible to win.

What You Get When You
Mix Up Breeds

Those of us who work in rescue have very strong intuitions about breed identification. It's not surprising that feeling competent about this is important to us—after all, when you've got a lot of brain space taken up with knowing how to tell a Norwich terrier from a Norfolk, you want to feel that that knowledge is important.

But even if you have entire breed books memorized, once purebreds start mixing, all bets are off. Yes, there are some extreme types that aren't going to show up by accident—the modern pug or bulldog, say, will never happen randomly. But only a tiny percent of a dog's genes are concerned with appearance—less than 1 percent of over 20,000. So a puppy could get half of its genes from, say, a collie parent, and still miss out on any of the distinctive visual features of that breed. And the features that scream, say, "Lab," are part of the general canine genome, so pure coincidence could easily bring together a short black coat, floppy ears, and a desire to chase balls, even if neither parent is a Labrador retriever.

If you find this hard to believe, you can try for yourself. The photo on the following page is one of many we could have used. It's a picture that's worth a million journal articles. Are these dogs pit bulls? Can you guess their breeds?

Their owner, Kristen Auerbach, says that people often ask

whether Otter and Fern are littermates. The answer is no, and in fact they are mixes of entirely different breeds. Otter, on the left, DNA tested as the offspring of a boxer/keeshond mix and an Australian cattle dog mix. Fern, on the right, tested as having one parent who was an American English coonhound and the other a Staffordshire terrier mix.

So, even setting aside the fact that we're always assuming that one or both parents are purebred when they could be the product of mixes going a long way back, the odds are pretty terrible that appearance is going to obviously reflect a dog's ancestry. And now that we have DNA analysis, we can actually test how often our guesses beat the odds. The studies show that we are fooled most of the time, as we'll see in the next section.

Guessing Breeds Is a Losing Game

Multiple studies have been done comparing people's guesses about a dog's breed from its looks to DNA testing with mixed-breed dogs. The results would be uniformly hilarious, if it weren't for the consequences this can have for pit bull types.

One study showed video clips of 20 dogs to 900 people with various kinds of dog experience, including veterinary medicine, sheltering, and dog clubs. For fourteen of the dogs, fewer than 50 percent of the participants identified a breed that matched the dog's DNA results.

Detailed examination of the wrong answers is also interesting. There was very little agreement among observers—only seven of the dogs got the same guesses from more than 50 percent of subjects. And even where people agreed, that didn't make it right—for three of those seven dogs, the breed the majority agreed on was wrong. So, even if everyone in the shelter staff is sure something is a beagle mix, apparently that doesn't prove a thing.

Another study compared breed identifications assigned by adoption agencies to DNA tests. Out of twenty dogs in the study, sixteen had been labeled as mixes of one or two specific breeds. Those guesses were partially correct for only four of those dogs, and only very partially. For three of the dogs, the correctly guessed breed was only 12.5 percent—just one grandparent—and the breeds of other three grandparents identified by DNA were totally missed. In one other dog, the guessed breed was found as a minor component of the dog's ancestry. So, in total in that study, the guesses corresponded to some part of the dog's actual heritage for only 31 percent of the dogs.

Finally, another study directly addressed what most concerns us here. This one was specifically about pit bulls. When four staff at each of four shelters guessed the supposed breed of a set of 120 dogs, they called sixty-two of the dogs some kind of pit bull. DNA tests were then conducted on all 120 dogs. You can guess where this is going at this point, right? Only twenty-five of the dogs

turned out to have any pit bull ancestry. One in three dogs with no pit bull in their DNA were identified as a pit bull by at least one staff member. What's more, one in five of the dogs with pit bull in their DNA had not been identified as such—which means they'd missed 20 percent of the actual pit bulls.

We're not trying to make fun of people who label the dogs at shelters. That's just where most of the studies have been done. And it's worth noting that DNA analysis of dogs is not yet perfect (and probably never will be). But all of this high-tech testing simply confirms what anyone can see by observation from a litter of puppies of known parents. No matter your depth of experience, none of us can accurately guess what a mixed breed dog is made of by looking at it.

You might actually be sad to think that your pit bull might not be a "real" pit bull after all. Don't be, though, because the good and bad news is that given the stereotypes and the legal issues that affect them these days, what matters is what *looks* like a pit bull, not papers. If your dog has got that bully look, whether it's fair or makes sense, we're all in this together. And that's the definition of *pit bull* that we'll be using for the rest of this book.

CHAPTER 2

how we saw pit bulls then

L et's play fill-in-the-blank. What dog breed is being talked about in this newspaper column?

Once more headlines blared last Saturday of another tiny tot, a four-year-old lad of Philadelphia being torn and mangled to death by a so-called wild dog. This happens some place in the country almost every day.

The dog in Saturday's horrible killing was, yes, as almost always, a _____.

Yet, we go on permitting this dangerous, slinky breed to multiply and run at large . . .

Think twice before buying a _____. If you do not have children, your neighbors may have. Keep a rattlesnake instead. It will give a warning, at least.

The answer? German shepherd, of course. You probably thought "pit bull," but that's because we weren't playing fair. If the writing style didn't clue you in, we should have told you that this column was from the year 1947. That would have been a big hint that "pit bull" was the wrong answer. It wasn't until the 1980s that the pit bull became notorious—and it was only the latest in a long line of breeds to hold that position.

Not What the Dog Does, but Who He Does It To

Karen Delise of the National Canine Research Council dove deep into decades of newspaper archives looking for articles about dogs for her book *The Pit Bull Placebo*. Her research showed that different eras have singled out different breeds as the scariest, and these changing reputations probably tell us more about ourselves than about dogs.

In America, the story goes back at least as far as the late nineteenth century, the heyday of the bloodhound, where Delise was struck by the familiarity of what she found. "The parallel to dogs labeled as pit bulls today was so profound," she says. "Here was a dog whose whole reputation was based almost 100 percent on what it was used for at the time."

Bloodhounds were bred for their skill at tracking by scent and were commonly used for finding people. But what people and

why? To a dog, the job is the same regardless, but to humans, who they're looking for makes all the difference. Everyone can agree that finding a lost child or a dangerous criminal is a good deed. But how about tracking escaped slaves? That depended on whose side you were on. And as opinions about slavery changed, so did the reputation of the dog.

As sympathy turned away from the slave owners who were tracking down their human property, these dogs became a symbol in popular media of the terrors their captives endured. In the second half of the nineteenth century, popular plays based on the book *Uncle Tom's Cabin* employed live bloodhounds in dramatic scenes of slaves being pursued. Seeing the effect of these scenes on the audience, producers used them for publicity, depicting them on posters and playbills, and displaying the actual dogs outside theaters between shows to attract attention. Given the widespread success of these plays, they were basically the equivalent of a viral media sensation: One scholar estimates that over 3 million people saw some staged version of *Uncle Tom's Cabin* between the years 1852 and 1930.

Since the slaves were the sympathetic characters at this point, the dogs were of course the bad guys. But, as Delise points out, nothing had changed about the dog or what it was doing—identifying a scent and following it to its source. "They were doing the exact same function—hunting a person—but with the label on the person, was the person good or bad, the

whole perception of the dog changed," she says. "If the dog finds a lost child, it's a hero. If the dog finds a runaway slave and bites him, he became a monster. We had a whole cultural shift and the dog just got caught up in the cultural shift. It's the same animal, but our perception changed."

Another interesting parallel to the pit bull of today that Delise found was that the term *bloodhound* referred more to a type of dog than a particular registered breed. "Any dog that put its nose to the ground, chased somebody, or followed somebody, were all labeled as bloodhounds. That included sometimes other purebreds, but mostly just mixes."

Fanciers of the purebred that we know as the bloodhound today defended it as being noble and gentle rather than savage and bloodthirsty. But this was a losing battle when other bloodhound-type dogs were specifically trained to behave aggressively—for example, the dogs were used by Spanish conquistadors against native populations in the New World, and by the United States against Native Americans being driven from their tribal lands, and during the Civil War both sides used them to hunt enemy soldiers.

While bloodhounds are rarely seen today, they were more common in the nineteenth century, and this was vital to their reputation. The most feared dog at a given time is always a fairly common, well-known breed, for a number of practical and psychological reasons. Partly it's that when a dog gets very popular, there are more dogs that are poorly bred and more owners may have picked that breed for the wrong reasons. Partly it's probably that sometimes society needs a monster, and it's not much use to have a monster we never get to see and talk about. But in large part it's just the logic of numbers. If a breed is uncommon, few people have enough experience of it for it to develop any particular reputation. So, nowadays, probably hardly anyone has an opinion one way or the other about whether bloodhounds are particularly dangerous, whereas everybody and their neighbor will have something to say about pit bulls.

Good Stereotypes vs. Bad

The American Kennel Club (AKC) registered its first German shepherd in 1908, and if you track its reputation over the rest of the century, there's probably no better example of how the exact same breed can be both a hero and villain, given enough dogs and enough appearances in the media.

By the 1920s, the German shepherd was starting to become both very popular and very unpopular at the same time. Delise quotes opinions calling them "treacherous, deceitful and vicious," and references to their alleged wolf blood were common. Don't forget that in those days, claiming that the German shepherd, say, had "only a thin veneer over the wolf" was not meant as a compliment. It's only quite recently that people wear T-shirts of howling wolves and find them mystical and profound—in previous centuries, in a less urbanized world, wolves were despised and feared as a danger to valuable livestock and to people.

In fact, one early proposed breed ban in the United States was on the German shepherd. In 1925, a New York city magistrate proposed that it should be illegal to own one in the city, saying that they were responsible for the majority of "hundreds" of bites. And in 1929, Australia made it illegal to import German shepherds, although breeding of the small population already in the country continued. The restriction was not completely lifted until 1979.

But in the United States, a few things happened at the same

time to counteract this trend in their reputation. In 1928, a blind man named Morris Frank returned from Germany with the first guide dog for the blind ever seen in the United States, a German shepherd named Buddy. Frank went on to cofound The Seeing Eye guide dog school, and while now retrievers are now more commonly trained for this work, for many years the German shepherd was the iconic guide dog. It's hard to brand an entire breed as monstrous against such an image of selfless service and devotion.

Another big contributor to the positive side of the scale was a movie superstar: German shepherd Rin Tin Tin, who debuted in 1922. The original Rin Tin Tin not only played a heroic dog in the movies but had a dramatic personal backstory: He was rescued as a blind, still nursing puppy from the bombed-out ruins of a German encampment during World War I.

As Susan Orlean tells it in *Rin Tin Tin: The Life and the Legend*, in the days of silent films, it wasn't unusual for a dog to be the main character in a movie—after all, the fact that you couldn't hear them speak was no problem. In fact, Rin Tin Tin wasn't the only German shepherd movie star in the 1920s. He was preceded by a famous dog named Strongheart, and there were actually over fifty German shepherds working in the movies at the time.

But Rin Tin Tin eclipsed them all. Soon after the premiere of his first movie *Where the North Begins*, thousands of fan letters started to arrive at the movie studio. Reviews treated him like any other actor. The poet Carl Sandburg wrote a review of the film, in which he referred to Rin Tin Tin as "a beautiful animal, he has the power of expression in his every movement that makes him one of the leading pantomimists of the screen."

Maybe the only time he was treated as second-class for being a dog was in 1927, when he got most votes for the first Best Actor Oscar, but the Academy decided it didn't like the impression that would give and gave the award to a human instead.

Rin Tin Tin gave birth to a character that outlived him. In 1946, 14 years after the first Rin Tin Tin died, before the release of a movie with Rin Tin Tin III, a nationwide survey claimed that he was the best-known motion picture personality ever. Of course, the survey was done by the studio making the movie, so perhaps it was a little biased, but it found that 70.3 percent of people knew his name, including children too young to have known the original in his lifetime.

Delise found that after some attacks by German shepherds in the 1940s, things were looking bad for the reputation of the breed again. But then, just like in the movies, Rin Tin Tin came to the rescue. A TV series debuted in 1954 and was an immediate success, with 9 million of the then 30 million TV sets in the nation tuning in to watch. This new TV fame put a shine on the breed's reputation but also contributed to a surge in popularity and resulting problems in the late 1960s and early '70s.

The truth is that any dog can act good or bad, regardless of breed, and for the German shepherd, the media reflected this truth, although in a kind of one-extreme-to-the-other way: both noble characters in the movies and "slinky" murderers in the news. "At the time there were lots of substandard, irresponsible owners, and they were extremely popular—they were being bred recklessly and used for all kinds of negative functions, and there were a lot of serious attacks and fatalities with German shepherds during their heyday," Delise says. "But because there seemed to be some kind of balance, it never disintegrated into the hatred and breed bashing that we see with pit bulls. There was this balance of seeing them do good work—dogs for the blind,

Rin Tin Tin, police dogs rescuing lost people—there was a lot positive press that helped balance all the irresponsible owners and attacks."

Lies, Damned Lies and Statistics

There have been too many breeds that went through a stage as the dangerous dog of the moment for us to go through them all here. Dobermans, once touted as intelligent, brave, and trainable, acquired a very different image when Hitler's troops used them in World War II. They attracted their own special myths, such as that their skulls were too small for their growing brain and this drove them mad. The rottweiler is another breed that had a somewhat briefer heyday as the iconic demonic dog fairly recently.

Still there are those that insist that this time, it's true—that pit bulls really are uniquely dangerous. But when sensational newspaper articles and websites make this claim, you need to think about where they get their numbers.

Let's think about what we'd need to prove that one breed bites more than another. First, we'd have to have some central agency collecting dog bites. No such thing exists, but the closest we can get are official Centers for Disease Control (CDC) statistics of emergency room visits. These statistics don't include information about breed, and with good reason. As we saw in Chapter 1, even dog experts are terrible at recognizing what is and isn't a pit bull or pit bull mix. And most people guessing what breed bit them aren't dog experts. So, the odds that we could get accurate information about breed in any dog bite is very low.

But let's say that by some miracle we did have that information—let's say, every dog that bit was legally required to have a DNA test. We'd also need to know how many pit bulls were in the population compared to other breeds. Let's take this down to small numbers that are easy to visualize: Say you have twenty pit bulls in your neighborhood and ten golden retrievers. Two pit bulls bite someone, and one golden bites someone. So, what do the statistics say about which breed is more likely to bite? Although there are twice as many pit bull bites, they are coming from twice as many pit bulls. So, the percentage of bites by dogs of both breeds is exactly the same. If those bites are predictive of future bites, you're exactly as likely to be bitten by a golden as by a pit bull.

So to know relative risk, we need to know how many dogs of what breeds are out there in the first place. We don't know that. There's no central registry of all the dogs everyone owns that says what breed or mix each one is; kennel club registries include only a fraction, and no mixed breeds. And let's say we somehow made this a legal requirement tomorrow: Everyone has to, say, put it on the national census form. The data would still be useless, because of the breed ID problem. We're hardly going to be able to force everyone to pay for a dog DNA test. So, a lot of the people who say their dogs are pit bulls would be wrong, and a lot of actual pit bulls would be called something else.

Pit Bull Attack! Film at 11!

And yet many people are sure pit bulls bite more. Why? Because you read about it in the news all the time! It must be true!

People who think this way don't understand how newspapers work. Not every dog bite makes the news. So, the number of newspaper articles about a certain breed tells us more about newspapers than it does about dogs.

"It's a very tiny sampling and it's not a random sampling," says Delise. "How does the media pick and choose the maybe 10 percent of severe dog attacks they report in the paper, which ones they report and which ones they don't? Sometimes it's probably are they busy that day—was there other news? What's the victim? It might be a sympathetic victim; it might not be a sympathetic victim. Who knows? But because we don't know, you can absolutely not use them as a source of statistics or information because we have no idea how they choose which cases they report and on what basis they choose."

Her research has shown us one thing that does attract coverage, though: When those two pit bulls and one golden bite someone, the pit bulls will be the ones to make the news.

Delise found over and over again that reports of attacks by pit bulls made much bigger news than reports of attacks by other breeds. One of many examples comes from September 2003, when a boy was killed by husky-type dogs in Alaska, an incident that was covered briefly in two Alaska newspapers. In December of the same year, the case of an elderly woman killed by what was reported as "a pack of pit bulls" in Florida was covered by over 200 US newspapers and TV stations, and appeared in newspapers in Australia, the United Kingdom, South Africa, and Canada.

And as should not surprise you at this point, many of the "pit bulls" in the widely covered news stories were cases of mistaken identification. In the widely publicized 2001 case of the fatal attack in San Francisco that killed Diane Whipple, the dogs were initially identified as pit bulls, although they were eventually correctly identified as Presa Canario. Still, Delise found that not everyone got the message, as often happens with newspaper corrections—later articles sometimes still called them pit bulls.

As noted earlier, nowadays breeds are defined by appearance rather than behavior, so that a pit bull is whatever someone thinks looks like a pit bull. But Delise's work shows that there does seem to be an exception to this: To some people, the way you know a dog is a pit bull is that it bites someone.

Let's Try Science

So, we can't get good data from newspapers, and we can't collect good epidemiological data because of the problems with breed ID and not knowing the percentage of different breeds in the population. Does that mean there's no way to know whether some breeds are more aggressive than others?

Researchers have actually done controlled studies of this question in various ways, and none of it points a finger at pit bulls as being an exceptionally human-aggressive breed.

A 2008 study published in *Applied Animal Behaviour Science* surveyed the owners of more than thirty breeds of dogs using a survey called C-BARQ that has been scientifically validated as a reliable assessment of a dog's typical behavior in a variety of situations. Questions about both human-directed and dog-directed aggression were analyzed separately.

The breeds with the highest percentage of dogs showing serious aggression toward people were dachshunds, Chihuahuas, Jack Russell terriers, Australian cattle dogs, American cocker spaniels, and beagles. Pit bulls did show higher levels of aggression towards other dogs (*not* humans), but they were only one of the breeds that stood out on this score. This was also true of Akitas, boxers, Australian cattle dogs, German shepherds, Chihuahuas, dachshunds, English springer spaniels, Jack Russell terriers, and West Highland white terriers.

Another study with a different methodology followed thirty-seven pit bulls and forty dogs of a similar size adopted from the same shelter. One pit bull and ten of the other dogs were returned to the shelter because of reported aggression. Of the dogs that were kept for at least two months, owner reports of aggressive behavior were similar for the two groups. They did find a few differences:

> The number of dogs reported to have displayed aggression towards their owner was 0 of the 23 pit bulls and 3 of the 21 dogs of other breeds.
>
> Three dogs in the Other Breeds group, but none in the Pit Bull group, had bitten their owners with enough force to break the skin. One pit bull and three other dogs were reported to have bitten a stranger, with only one of the bites (by a dog in the Other Breeds group) severe enough to break the skin.

And finally:

> Reported care of the two groups was also similar except that pit bulls were more likely to sleep on the owner's bed and more likely to cuddle with the owner.

The authors of the study, as all good authors of studies do, suggest that their results should be treated with caution. For

instance, although this shelter had no formal temperament testing at the time, it got dogs from other shelters where pit bull adoptions were banned, and those shelters likely did some pre-screening, only sending on the best dogs. But even so, if pit bulls were overwhelmingly more dangerous than other dogs, you'd expect to see some effect of this.

One last example for now: In Lower Saxony, Germany, a law was passed in the early 2000s restricting ownership of a number of breeds deemed inherently dangerous. Dogs of these breeds had to pass a temperament test to avoid euthanasia or else to be exempt from a requirement to wear a muzzle, depending on which breed. The breeds included American Staffordshire terriers, bull terriers, dogs of the pit bull type, and Staffordshire bull terriers. Of the specified breeds, 415 dogs were tested . . . and 95 percent showed no aggression. In a later study, a control group of seventy golden retrievers were tested, and no significant difference in aggression was found. As a result, the legislation was changed and no longer referred to a list of specific breeds.

Nature and Nurture

Everyone who works with dogs has strong intuitions about the typical temperament of different breeds and types of dogs and we can all cite tons of anecdotes to back us up. The problem is that given the way the human mind works, we have to be skeptical about using this as evidence. We all have a tendency to see what we expect and to remember what fits with the stories we already tell ourselves. We remember the hounds that were obsessed with sniffing and ignored us when we called them, and forget about the ones that were all up in our face for the treat. We don't keep a running tally in our mind to add up and compare to the stereotypes—we mostly just forget the exceptions.

And even when we try to use the scientific method to get around this, it's a hard thing to study in a controlled way, because survey research is subject to the same problem. People tend to see their own dogs through the same lens of breed, and may notice and report the breed-specific traits that they are expecting more than the others that they are not.

But even so, the evidence of such studies suggests we need to pay attention to individual dogs and not expect identifying the breed to do all the work for us.

There are definitely some very specific behaviors that can be and have been selected for by breeding in working breeds. Border collies, for example, have been bred to exaggerate one part of this, called the "eye-stalk," which you can easily see if you watch one working sheep. But this requires very careful selection for particular behaviors, and as noted earlier, most modern breeding concentrates on appearance. In fact, when working breeds are newly proposed for inclusion in a registry such as the AKC, this usually starts a war among fanciers—some breeders will fight it, saying that working ability will be compromised once dogs are being bred for a "beauty contest." The result is that in many recognized breeds, such as retrievers, there are separate lines, with some people still breeding for working ability (behavior) and others concentrating on winning conformation shows (the "beauty contests").

These specific working traits aren't of much relevance to what most of us are looking for in a pet, though, since our main priority isn't usually, say, retrieving dead ducks. But there have also been studies of behavioral traits that are of more interest to companion dog owners, and some show that the original functions of breeds don't correlate highly with these traits, either. One large study in Sweden in 2005 looked at 13,097 dogs of 31 breeds for four traits: playfulness, curiosity/fearlessness, sociability, and aggressiveness. Breeds did differ on these measures, but the differences were not correlated with their traditional uses—for instance, all types of herding breeds or terriers, say, didn't show the same scores. Looking at retrievers, for example, Labs ranked as number one on the trait curiosity/fearlessness while goldens were twenty-sixth out of the thirty-one breeds.

OK, but what about the trait everyone's worried about in pit bulls: aggression?

First of all, we need to separate out human-directed and dog-directed aggression. As we saw in the 2008 study cited earlier, the tendency to aggression toward dogs and toward people wasn't necessarily correlated—some breeds in that studied showed one and not the other. Diane Jessup says that this is particularly true in dogs bred for fighting, where aggression toward humans is the opposite of what you want. "If you look at pictures of dog fighting, the handlers are down on the ground next to the dog, inches from them, urging them on." She says she's never been bitten breaking up fights between her dogs over the years "because they do not redirect their aggression toward humans. In the pit, where there's three other people in there, they cannot get stupid and bite out at a human."

Focusing then specifically on human-directed aggression, there are cases that provide evidence that this can have a genetic component. One of them is a breed that is rarely mentioned in these discussions: It's the springer spaniel. A couple of studies found that this is the breed most frequently referred to behavioral specialists for aggression, in numbers that can't be accounted for by breed popularity—the rate is high given the number of dogs of the breed. The studies also found a connection to a particular bloodline, which strongly suggests a genetic component.

If there's a genetic component, then it's possible to breed both for and against human-directed aggression—and as Jessup observes, this is a trait that would have been specifically selected against in fighting dogs. So, if anything, its background as a

Thinking About Risk

When Deirdre adopted her first dog, Carla Lou, she found it challenging to fully trust that Carla was the gentle, loving dog that she presented herself to be. She would look at Carla Lou and wonder whether Carla would turn on her while she slept. What if she rolled over onto Carla and it triggered something from her past? These irrational fears disappeared once she picked up Janice Bradley's book *Dogs Bite: But Balloons and Slippers Are More Dangerous*, which taught her that your bedroom dresser and house slippers are far more risky than dog ownership.

There's no agency that officially keeps track of all dog bites, but the most reliable source is the CDC system that tracks emergency room visits. What we see from this data first of all is that the number of dog bites is not increasing. It's been staying the same, somewhere around 330,000, despite the increasing population of the United States, which suggests that proportionally the risk is actually going down. And while that may seem like a largish number, there are estimated to be 69,926,000 pet dogs in the United States and a human population of around 319 million, so that's actually an awful lot of not-biting going on.

The next thing we see is that the vast majority of those reported bites—96 percent—are minor, with patients being treated and released. This is a high proportion of minor injuries compared to other causes, because people are more likely to see a doctor for a dog bite than a similar injury with say, a knife. This means that comparisons to statistics for other causes of injury can be a bit misleading, making the risk of serious injury seem higher than it is.

Since many dog bites are so minor that they are not reported or treated, a couple of studies tried to estimate the number of total dog bites via a random telephone survey rather than medical records. When you see a larger number quoted than the one above for total yearly dog bites, it comes from one of these studies—a total of around 4.5 million, for example, from the more recent one conducted from 2001 to 2003. That number can also be misleading unless you understand that the survey even counted bites that didn't break the skin.

While none of the statistics are perfect, given the best numbers we can get, how dangerous are dogs compared to other things we commonly encounter in everyday life? People can get hurt by scissors, too, but no one goes around suggesting that we ban scissors.

The comparison in Bradley's title comes from the United Kingdom, where they conveniently break down injury records into very specific causes. For the years 2000–2002, there were slightly more injuries caused by slippers (64,974) than by dogs (62,743). And slippers were actually the safest sort of footwear—the numbers for sneakers and shoes were higher (214,646 and 198,670, respectively).

So, why aren't people more afraid of sneakers than of dogs? Human beings are pretty terrible at estimating risk in general, and dog bites have several qualities that are known to make us even worse at judging how dangerous something is. We feel less risk if we're in control, and if a strange dog runs up to you, you're not in control. Something that poses a danger to children seems scarier to us than something that only affects adults, which is understandable, since protecting one's offspring is heavily selected for in evolution.

But evolution has also prepared us pretty badly for the modern world. "We didn't evolve in an environment where the world was full of two-ton balls of rolling metal, but we did evolve in an environment where there was a significant risk of large predators with big sharp teeth," says Bradley. So, we're less afraid to put our children in a car—one of the most dangerous things we can expose them to—than we are of them being bitten by a strange dog.

fighting dog should make us less afraid of being bitten by a pit bull, not more.

Genes and Environment

It's not an accident that the previous section is titled "Nature *and* Nurture," not *or*. "Nature or nurture" is not a question that makes sense. Everything about behavior is a combination of both genetics and environment.

If you read the modern advice on raising puppies, it puts a big emphasis on proper socialization. And this doesn't mean the colloquial definition of that word—we're not suggesting you take your puppy to cocktail parties. It means that during the critical period of development, your puppy needs to be exposed to everything you want it to be comfortable with in everyday life.

This is critical because genes only provide a starting point. As the Coppingers put it, "Good dogs are made after they are born, not before." The shepherds they studied knew that. Picking the dogs with the right behavioral tendencies was only the start. Then the dogs needed to be raised with the flock so that during the critical developmental period, they learn that sheep are their social group, not their prey. No matter how great the genes, if the dog wasn't raised right, it wouldn't grow up to be a good livestock guard. The ultimate behavior of the dog is a combination of genes and environment even in these dogs that are selected for inherited behavior much more rigorously than our pets are.

Early experience affects the developing brain. Certainly dogs are born with different temperaments, but how they are raised affects the expression of those traits. Dogs that are innately shy, for example, may never fling themselves into the arms of every passing stranger, no matter how they are raised. But with proper socialization they can at least be comfortable in a variety of situations. And if for some crazy reason you actually wanted a dog that was shy or fearful, there's no need to breed for it. You can much more easily create that by taking just about any puppy and making sure it's isolated from normal life during its development. As we'll discuss in Chapter 5, how a dog is kept is the biggest risk factor for whether it's a danger to people.

And that's perhaps the biggest reason that concentrating on breed doesn't make us safer and a particular breed is the wrong thing to fear: We can make any dog into a monster, and it's not by breeding.

CHAPTER 3

how we see
pit bulls now

Hearing all the stories of famous American pit bulls from the early twentieth century, you might wonder, how did we get from the point where the pit bull was every boy's best friend to one where it is seen as something to be feared?

To start, we need to recognize that that question is an oversimplification. The pit bull's image has always been somewhat ambiguous. There's a reason this dog was used as a symbol in war: The point was to convey that we had the strength to win. When you're facing a dangerous enemy, you need that willingness and ability to fight. But inevitably, those qualities can have a dark side.

You and Me Against a Dangerous World

That double-edged sword was more accepted in the past because the world was a different place, one where physical strength and bravery were more necessary qualities—and we were in it together with our dogs.

In her historical research that we referred to in Chapter 2, Karen Delise observed that in nineteenth-century America, the dogs then referred to bulldogs were often praised for their fierceness. These days, people deciding on a pet aren't usually looking for the word *fierce* in the breed description. But these dogs were more than pets—they had work to do. On the frontier or farm, they often served as protection from wildlife and even our own livestock, as in one 1907 news article that Delise found:

> Twenty women, including the bulldog's owner, all summer boarders, were picking huckleberries on Prospect Hill yesterday. At the top of the berry patch is a pasture. The bull in it suddenly became ferocious, broke through the light fence and charged the berry pickers.
>
> Their skirts and the brush impeded their flight, but the bulldog rushed uphill, met the bull half way, caught its nose and held on like grim death. The dog's weight threw the bull on the steep descent; over and over they rolled and brought up against a fence

at the bottom of the hill. The impact parted them. The bull, with
wounded nostrils, ran away; the dog, wagging its stubby tail, ran
to its owner.

"Good dog! Good dog!" chorused twenty women, smoothing their
skirts and the dog's hide.

So, to be fierce wasn't a negative trait, Delise writes: "Fierceness was associated with courage and fortitude, and these characteristics were needed on farms, in the wilderness, and even cities." This word was never used in terms of aggression toward humans, and was distinct from calling a dog (or a bull) ferocious or vicious. In fact, dogs were often described as fierce when reported protecting their humans from attacks by "ferocious" or "mad" dogs.

In fact, bloodthirstiness would have been a disqualification for the pit bull's ancestral jobs. As hunting dogs, their skill was to grip and hold large wild game, such as a boar or stag, until hunters caught up and killed it. They were also used in the same way by butchers and farmers to control cattle—which city folk may not realize are big, dangerous animals that even nowadays sometimes kill people working with them. But while these tasks called for a dog with strength and determination, it couldn't have the desire to maim or kill another animal—not when that animal was a valuable resource in its own right.

Defense, Not Offense

Still, people saw the dark side of these qualities even in the days when they had their uses, so there probably have been people maligning pit bulls for as long as there have been pit bulls, and owners defending them. The defenses were different than they might be today, though. Of course the pit bulls were admired for their loyalty and intelligence and everything else we praise in a dog nowadays. But rather than saying that their dogs were not fighters, the defense was more that they only used their powers for good, and not evil. No one felt any need to make excuses for a dog's standing up for himself against another dog, as long as he didn't pick the fight in the first place.

One eloquent example of this comes from the writings of James Thurber, well known for his cartoons that often included dogs. The most familiar canine in his cartoons is more or less a bloodhound (another dog with a mixed reputation, as we saw in Chapter 2) but in 1935 he wrote movingly of a real dog he had as a child, Rex: "He was a bull terrier. 'An American bull terrier,' we used to say, proudly; none of your English bulls." Thurber relates anecdotes of Rex's cheerful feats of strength—playing fetch with a 10-foot wooden rail, and coming home one night dragging a chest of drawers. He also writes matter-of-factly of Rex's run-ins with other dogs:

He was a tremendous fighter, but he never started fights. He never went for a dog's throat but for one of its ears (that teaches a dog a lesson), and he would get his grip, close his eyes, and hold on. He could hold on for hours. His longest fight lasted from dusk to almost pitch-dark, one Sunday.

Rex's joy of battle, when battle was joined, was almost tranquil. He had a kind of pleasant expression during fights, his eyes closed in what would of seemed to be sleep had it not been for the turmoil of the struggle. The Fire Department finally had to be sent for and a powerful stream of water turned on the dogs for several moments before Rex finally let go.

The Thurber boys had to deal with pit bull prejudice, but to them, the fact that Rex only used his strength for defense, not offense, made all the difference:

The story of that Homeric fight got all around town, and some of our relatives considered it a blot on the family name. They insisted we get rid of Rex, but nobody could have made us give him up. We would have left town with him first. It would have been different, perhaps, if he had ever looked for trouble. But he had a gentle disposition. He never bit a person in the ten strenuous years that he lived, nor ever growled at anyone except prowlers.

Double-Edged Swords

Rex sounds like exactly the dog you'd want with you on the frontier or in the trenches of World War I. But strength can also be used in cruel ways, and human nature being what it is, that was bound to happen as well—turning the holding of bulls into a blood sport, and eventually setting dogs against each other.

It's worth remembering that those sports have their roots in a time where life wasn't much more humane for people, either. We don't set dogs against bears or bulls anymore for fun, just as we don't attend the hangings of criminals or burn alleged witches in the town square.

But times change and our attitudes toward animals have changed enormously in the last century. One thing this led to was, in the 1970s, a big effort to stamp out dogfighting. You'd think that would only be good news, but—as with everything concerning pit bulls—it turned out to be more complicated than that.

How the Pit Bull Became a Monster

Dogfighting has been made illegal more than once in the last few centuries. But laws are only effective when enforced—which these mostly weren't.

For a long time, the participants weren't necessarily people we'd think of as criminals, but men with respected positions: lawyers, businessmen, and even police. In the first half of the twentieth century, books and magazines about fighting dogs were openly published with ads for dogs for sale and reports of fights with results, like the next-day news stories of any other sport. One famous breeder, Joseph Colby, published a book in 1936 that along with history and breeding info, included chapters on preparing dogs for a fight and caring for them afterward. There were also a number of chapters on great dogs with play-by-play descriptions of famous fights. So, there was a time when dogfighting, although it may have been technically illegal, went on without even being particularly underground.

Whatever you think of their sport, these men were clearly devoted to their dogs, but eventually, changing views of humane treatment of animals overtook them. You might think this would have been 100 percent good news for dogs, but the way things played out, there were unintended consequences.

Pits Become Big News

In the 1970s, anti-dogfighting campaigns began to make big news, and in 1976, dogfighting was made a federal crime. Arresting dogfighters and confiscating their dogs—how could there be downsides to that? Well, one was that widespread media coverage spread a terrifying image of these dogs. The other was that the very organizations that were supposed to be helping dogs were part of the problem.

News coverage that grabs for eyeballs with sensationalism and wild headlines is not a creation of the Internet age. A photo of a crazed-looking dog could grab a lot of attention in the days when magazine covers were displayed on newsstands for all to see. And editors have always been good at picking attention-getting headlines, giving us such titles as "A Boy and His Dog in Hell" (*Rolling Stone*) and "Time Bomb on Legs" (*Time*). These articles also included sensational myths that had no basis in reality—myths you still hear repeated today, including totally fictional numbers about the bite force of a pit bull and the claim that they can lock onto something with their front teeth and chew with the back.

Often these alleged facts are unattributed, but worse, where they have sources, they are citing as coming from legitimate animal experts. You can't blame reporters for writing that pit bulls have locking jaws when they got that tidbit from publications of the Humane Society of the United States (HSUS). And the title "Time Bomb on Legs" is actually a direct quote in the article attributed to the dean of the Tufts University veterinary school.

With extensive coverage of this sort, at least some of which cited apparently legitimate experts, it's no wonder that many people—who may never have given a thought to pit bulls before—came to believe that these dogs were uniquely monstrous. And sadly, it may even have supplied crueler ideas to dogfighters. This is also the period when the myth started that dogs were trained on "bait dogs" and other animals, such as kittens. Reading books from Colby's period, nothing like this is mentioned as part of the training regimen; author Bronwen Dickey finds that it's also not found anywhere in the underground fighting literature. In fact, the likelihood is that if bait dogs are ever used in modern times, it's because people got the idea from news coverage.

There's a lot more than can be said about this period and the societal factors that contributed to the image of pit bulls. The changing demographics of dogfighting in this period gave these dogs an association with inner-city crime that they didn't have before and added an element of racial prejudice to breed prejudice. And Vicki Hearne made the observation that this was a time when our attitudes toward fighting itself changed—protests against the Vietnam War put nonviolence to the fore as a virtue in a way it hadn't been earlier in the century, when we felt we were fighting just wars. These and other factors—none of which were based on hands-on experience in reality with actual dogs—conspired to give pit bulls an over-the-top reputation for violence.

With Friends like These . . .

Myths were not the worst of what started in this period, though. It began a long period when many animal shelters adopted policies forbidding the adoption of pit bulls—instead, they were euthanized purely on the basis of what they looked like.

As Deirdre related in her book *Little Darling's Pinups for Pitbulls*, her own story began in a shelter like this, when a woman came in with a lost dog. Informed that it would be automatically euthanized immediately because it looked like a pit bull, Deirdre asked to take it home, but her request was denied. Despite con-

tacting rescues, she couldn't save that dog, but that effort led to her adopting another dog sight unseen from Texas, and then to a career fighting breed-specific policies and prejudice.

Change Trickles Up

Fortunately, even in the 1980s, not everyone working in animal welfare went along with the party line. Jane Berkey started Animal Farm Foundation (AFF) in 1985, intending to run a horse rescue. Around the same time she went to a shelter to adopt a dog, and just happened to pick a pit bull. The experience of living with that dog changed her plans.

"She couldn't believe how much she and her dog were being discriminated against even though neither of them had ever done anything wrong," says AFF executive director Stacey Coleman.

There were plenty of horse rescues but few, if any, that focused on pit bulls. Seeing the need, Berkey changed the organization's mission. She pulled dogs from shelters to rehab and adopt them out, and even took in dogs from fighting busts, viewing them as victims of animal cruelty rather than some kind of genetic mutation. But Berkey quickly realized that more was needed than saving individual dogs.

"As she learned more about the issues, she learned that she couldn't possibly run enough dogs through a rescue to make a lasting impact," says Coleman. "That's when she started the educational aspect of the foundation."

AFF's education efforts set a precedent for other small groups to follow, but the foundation faced the struggle of getting its message out when national organizations were saying something very different. Coleman thinks that the moment when things really started to turn around was the high-profile dogfighting bust of football player Michael Vick in 2007.

One reason the Vick case made such an impact was probably that it presented an almost mythic story—a clear villain and his innocent victims. In any case, suddenly there was a moment that the public was on the side of these dogs.

"We had the opportunity to take that momentum of public sentiment," says Coleman. And she says that the fact this moment came out of a dogfighting case opened a way to fighting the stereotype differently. After years of bad publicity, pit bulls were inextricably associated in the public mind with dogfighting, no matter that only a tiny fraction of the dogs had ever been anywhere near a ring. Now, rather than fight the losing battle to break that association, they could just go with it; instead, show the public that dogs that came from dogfighting weren't scary after all.

As Coleman recalls it, this was a harder sell to the larger organizations working on the Vick bust than it was for the public. She remembers calling one representative of HSUS on the phone: "I said, 'I don't trust you and you don't trust me, but we've got to get past this. Let's agree to listen to each other and see what we can come up with.'" And they got past it, resulting in a change that gave all fight-bust dogs a second chance. "It was a rich moment in history when animal welfare finally agreed that even if some of them didn't believe that the dogs were going to make pet material, they at least deserved the opportunity because they were in fact victims of animal cruelty."

Changing Perspective

The rescue of the Vick dogs may have changed public opinion, but even an organization like Animal Farm Foundation, which had been working for these dogs from the beginning, still had something to learn along the way.

"It's not like Animal Farm has a history that's free of buying into stereotypes, because that's how we started," Coleman says. "When she started, the old mythology ruled the day. We didn't think there was something wrong with the dogs, but we hadn't taken it to the next level to identify what the actual challenge was."

Coleman can pinpoint the moment that her thinking shifted. She was in her office, overhearing the discussion at a retreat AFF was hosting for staff of a major animal welfare organization. Going around the room, the participants were relating experiences at a pit bull adoption promotion that hadn't been as successful as they were hoping.

"Every experience had to do with human perception and human prejudice," she recalls. "No one, not once, said that these

dogs are too hard to handle or the dogs aren't good or the dogs are scary. The challenges were never about the dogs. It was at that moment that I realized that we need to change the way we're talking about this and stop focusing on the dogs. There's nothing wrong with the dogs. Let's stop trying to fix something that's not broken, and let's start tackling the human prejudice that influences how we live with these dogs."

When AFF started, its founders knew that the stereotypes were wrong, but the unspoken assumption was that these were dogs that needed special help—that the dogs had to change. "We kept putting the responsibility on the dogs to exhibit the change we needed, instead of putting the responsibility on the humans to change old habits," Coleman says. "It was more about managing and training the dogs to be good dogs, because we weren't free of that bias yet."

Now AFF has refocused its education efforts for both the public and professionals.

"We do internships where people come from shelters and animal welfare organizations and come and stay with us for a week. They come thinking we're going to be learning about dog behavior, but they learn about human behavior more than anything." Coleman says there's an emphasis on helping people perceive dogs as individuals rather than members of a category. "You can tell as many anecdotes as you want about how your nice pit bull is, but it's still an anecdote. It's not more or less valid than someone who had a bad experience with a dog at some point. So, we had to start looking at the dogs as individuals and say, 'You had that bad experience with that particular dog, that must have been horrible for you, but this dog over here didn't do it, and you don't need to confuse the two.'"

This has changed the foundation's approach to rescue dogs as well, treating them more as individuals with varying individual needs. "Now that we approach adoptions that way, our dogs go home so quickly," says Coleman. AFF even has waiting lists for puppies. "They go home immediately. It's such a joy, because there were times years ago where it would take ages to find placements."

One Shelter's Story

When new CEO Lisa LaFontaine ended the pit bull euthanasia policy at the Washington Humane Society (WHS) in Washington, DC, in 2007, there was no big press conference, no special celebration for the first pit bull-type dog adopted out in many years.

"We just wanted to treat dogs as dogs, so we didn't scream it from the rooftops," she says.

Despite that matter-of-fact attitude about the goal, the change was a big deal. This was not only a shelter where all pit bulls were automatically euthanized—it was one where a previous director had even supported a proposed pit bull ban for the whole city. In a letter to the editor published in the *Washington Post* in 2000, Mary Healey did note that many pit bulls are the victims of "horrible abuse." But she also continued the bad old tradition of spreading the myths, writing that "most dogs bite and release; pit bulls bite, hold, grind and shake," and that "animal control officers know them to be especially unpredictable and aggressive."

LaFontaine's perspective was vastly different. Prior to joining the staff of the Washington shelter, she'd been CEO of Monadnock Humane Society in New Hampshire since 2000, where she'd started as a volunteer in 1997. Like WHS, it was an open admission shelter—one that had to take any animal that was brought to it—that also handled animal control. Unlike WHS, there, pit bulls were viewed no differently from other dogs.

"We treated every dog who came in the same way, and had extremely high adoption rates," LaFontaine recalls. "We saw lots of pit bull dogs—we saw lots of dogs of all kinds—so I was very used to working with them, sheltering them, adopting them, just treating them like normal dogs."

So, she already knew that if she ended up in the DC job, she'd change the policy against adopting out pit bulls. But then when she was there for an interview, something happened that made her all the more determined. She was being taken on a tour of the shelter's various facilities around the city when at one, a family was waiting in the lobby to surrender what looked like an energetic adolescent bully breed mix.

"He looked sort of boxer-y, very exuberant, pulling at the leash, not in an aggressive way, just very jumpy," she recalls. "That is very typical of what we see given up in a shelter—dogs that aren't puppies anymore and people haven't trained them."

She greeted the family and continued around the building. "Twenty minutes, maybe a half-hour into my tour, we were coming around in a circle back to the front lobby, and the dog's body was carried past me. The dog had been euthanized already and was on his way to the freezer."

The speed of the process astounded her. She asked if something in particular had been wrong with the dog that wasn't apparent to the eye, or was it always this quick. The answer was that this was the normal procedure. Strays legally had to be held for seven days, but owner-surrender pit bulls were walked immediately back to be euthanized.

"The thought went through my head: 'I have to get this job,'" she says. "That's the moment that I really wanted to fight for this role, so that I could undo that."

LaFontaine knew from her previous experience that a breed-neutral policy worked. But as anyone who works with both will tell you: animals are easy, it's people that are hard.

She had no idea how the staff and community would react to a different approach after years of being told that these dogs were uniquely dangerous. An event early on, though, gave her faith that change was going to be welcome. The Walk for Animals was a fund-raising event held on the National Mall, where about a thousand WHS supporters came and walked with their dogs. She greeted the stage to speak and looked out over the crowd, and what she saw made her believe that the community would support her.

"Despite the fact that the biggest animal welfare organization in the District has abandoned them and has been advocating against them and hasn't been adopting them out over the years, I see pit bulls everywhere in this crowd," she recalls. "And there's no stereotyping who they were with. Every age group, every socioeconomic group, every racial group, every demographic I could think of was represented on the other end of the leash."

And back at WHS, she found an organization that was ready for change at every level, from volunteers who'd left over the policy to the top management. "We had a group of board members who were really pained by the number of animals that were being euthanized by the organization," she says, and of course, a huge proportion of those were pit bulls. So, when LaFontaine announced her plan at a meeting of about a dozen senior staff, "You could see everyone's tentative exhale of, 'Wow, are we really going to do this?'"

They were, but it couldn't happen overnight, because if pit bulls were going to be treated like any other dog, every aspect of shelter operations would be affected. A few thousand extra dogs per year would now have to be handled with the same number of employees, from vets to kennel staff. Management took a couple of months to study and modify its procedures, but there was no getting around the fact that the change meant extra work. For the most part, though, the staff was happy to do it, because no one was hit harder by the old policy than they were. "For the strays who stayed for seven days, they were walking them, they were feeding them, they were caring for them, then they knew that they had to walk them to the euthanasia room at the end of the stray hold. So, they embraced the extra work because it meant life. It meant hope."

At first, people were still sometimes wary despite themselves, because the old ways were so ingrained. "For the most part I found a group of staff members and volunteers who desperately wanted to make this change, but they had been told for so many years that there was something wrong with these dogs," LaFontaine says. "There was a lot of history to undo in a very short period of time." She remembers the first litter of pit bull puppies under the new policy. "There was still this fear— 'Oh my God, we don't know what they're going to become.' I said, 'They're puppies. We never know what they're going to become.'"

But the change was positive not just for pit bulls, but for the organization as a whole. Life clearly changed enormously for the employees. Interviewed a few years later, the staff recalled clearly how difficult the old policy was for them. "It was painful. I cried plenty of days," said one; "It's not something you can just swallow or get used to. Mentally, you have to deal with it." They remembered falling in love with pit bulls that were then euthanized, and how heartbreaking it was to see this happen even to puppies. And their feelings when things changed? "I wanted to jump off the roof with joy," one said.

Volunteers and donors who'd left over the old policy came back, and people were more willing to come to adopt. And some changes helped other dogs as well. One of the first pit bulls that stayed in the shelter a long time ended up inspiring a program that continues to this day. Two staff members who were runners starting taking him on runs, and this turned into a group called PACK (People and Animal Cardio Klub). It's still going strong, and that dog had a happy ending, according to LaFontaine: "He got adopted and his owner ended up hiking the Appalachian trail with him."

WHS policy is now that pit bulls get no special treatment— no targeted adoption events, different temperament tests, or stricter adoption screening. But like many in the shelter community, LaFontaine can't help feeling that these dogs are special anyway. She believes that's part of how change got started at shelters in the first place.

"Anecdotally, there are a whole lot of people in the animal welfare community that have pit bulls," says LaFontaine, whose daughter has two and whose own dog is something like a pit bull-whippet cross. "Part of it is they're here and we see them and we fall in the love with them. Part of it is because they have qualities that are very lovable that cause us to advocate for them—loyalty and clowniness and energy and fun. I think that the people who work in organizations like mine, who care for them every day, who pick them out as the ones that they want to adopt in their family, have just sort of created this groundswell of voices advocating for them."

CHAPTER 4

pre-owned dogs

Lots of publicity for shelters and rescues basically amounts to "adopt so dogs don't die." It's hard to argue with that motivation, but we'd rather emphasize a different reason to adopt. There are a lot of great dogs out there looking for a home, and if you're interested in a pit bull type, there are tons to choose from.

The process can be daunting if you don't know what to expect, though, and people are often nervous about the potential problems of taking on a secondhand dog. In this chapter we'll talk about some things to know and to think about if you're considering adopting a pit bull.

Why Are Dogs Homeless?

There's a stereotype that shelter dogs are discarded and somehow defective. It's true that people who surrender dogs to rescue and shelters do often mention behavioral problems as part of their motivation. But remember that often one person's trash is another's treasure. Here are some reasons why a fear of behavioral problems shouldn't put you off the idea of adoption.

Bad behavior is in the eye of the beholder.

Research on why people give up their dogs has found again and again that it's often the result of a mismatch between an own-

er's expectations and the qualities of a particular dog—or even simply unrealistic expectations about owning a dog in general. One study showed that in nearly a third of cases, the reason for surrender was that the dog was more work than the owner expected. The fact that an owner made a bad choice or had no idea how much time it took to care for a pet is no reflection on the particular dog.

When it comes to behavior, dogs and people are all so different that the specifics are hugely important. To beagle lovers, the fact that their dogs howl is adorable, while to others, this might be sheer torture. Dogs are often surrendered for being too energetic, and how energetic you want your dog to be is a matter of opinion . . . and so on. Long story short, the wrong dog for one person is likely the perfect dog for someone else.

Bad behavior is situational.

One study found that only 20 percent of dogs adopted and returned were reported to have the same behavioral issue in more than one home. This isn't really surprising, because all behavior is a response to the situation the dog is in. In a home where a dog gets more exercise and chew toys, it won't be chewing up the furniture from boredom. In a home without a cat, you won't see it chasing the cat. And it's important to remember that a problem one person can't solve may be trivial for another. Study after study finds that many dogs are given up for housebreaking problems, which is a continuing mystery to dog trainers, who find that housetraining is not exactly rocket science.

Angela Keith of the Merit Pit Bull Foundation in North Carolina says that often when owners give a reason for surrender, "They see it as behavioral issues; we see it as, they really didn't give the dog what the dog needed." So if you're the person who can give that dog what it needs, the same problems are unlikely to be repeated.

It's not always about the dog.

Many dogs end up in rescue for reasons having little to do with the particular dog, and this is particularly true of pit bull types. People may give up a pit bull because they have to move to a place with a breed ban or can't find an apartment that allows them. Keith tells of one adopter who wept at returning his dog because of harassment from a neighbor who didn't want a pit bull in the neighborhood. "He was a great dog owner, he was happy with the dog," she says. "He couldn't take the pressure."

Personal problems and changes in the household are other common reasons to give up a dog. Some of these are beyond anyone's control, such as becoming too sick or disabled to care for a pet, or the death of the owner. Other reasons may seem pretty lame in the eyes of rescuers. "We get a lot of, 'We're separating and we can't decide who's going to take the dog'—that one always baffles me," says Keith. But you're not adopting the owner, you're adopting the dog, and this means a great dog is looking for a home for no fault of its own.

It's important to remember that people, especially those with limited resources, do give up dogs that they think are great dogs. One recent study of large dogs—including mostly pit bull types—surrendered to shelters in New York City and Washington, DC, found that this was a difficult decision for most people, and the reasons given were not purely behavioral:

Most people in our study took a long time to think before they relinquished the dog. The majority of people tried something to avoid relinquishing the dog, and they thought it was possible that something could have helped them keep their dog. Poignantly, when asked what they liked best about their dog, most responses were caring and demonstrated attachment. Responses included "dog is like a child to them" or "just loved him" or "he was always excited to see me." In addition, when asked what they would tell a new adopter, responses included comments like "she is affectionate and lies in bed with you" or "he is a good, loving dog" or "he will make you love him and pet him." Responses to this question often included specific likes or dislikes of the dog, such as "loves to have his belly rubbed" or "likes to watch TV."

So, the perfect dog for you may be out there, and it's your good luck that its first home didn't work out. Think about your needs and expectations, then work with a shelter or rescue that will help you meet the right dog for you.

Where to Adopt

Shelters and private rescues can be very different. Shelters are more like going online to find a date—you know only a little about each other to start, but there are a lot of choices. Rescues

are usually more like being introduced to a date by a friend of a friend—someone who knows something about the two of you thinks you may suit each other. Both ways to adopt work, but it helps to know what to expect going in.

Private rescues

Private rescues usually have dogs living in foster homes with volunteers. Every private rescue is different, but here are some basics to expect from a well-organized group:

- Expect to fill out a fairly long form. You may be asked about your current and former pets and be asked for vet references and sometimes personal references. The rescue will also want to be sure you're allowed to have a dog where you're living, and that there are no restrictions on pit bulls.
- Expect someone to talk to you on the phone about your written application once the initial processing is done.
- Many rescues do home visits. For most, these are mostly meant to be educational, especially if you've never had a dog before. It also helps the rescue figure out what kind of dog your home is suitable for—maybe your stairs would be hard for a dog with special needs or your fence is jumpable by certain dogs.
- The process may take several weeks—remember that these are volunteers with jobs and families, doing all of this in their spare time.

- Expect to sign a contract. Expect it to include a clause that if you can't keep the dog, you must return it to the rescue. This is the same as you'd expect from a responsible breeder. See it as a benefit—if the worst happens, there is somewhere for your dog to go.

People often make a fuss about feeling judged by the process of adopting from a rescue, but it's to your advantage for the rescue to have detailed information about you and your situation. Unlike in a shelter, the foster caregivers are living with the dogs and they know a lot about them, so this helps them make the right match.

To be fair, rescuers can get burned out and be judgmental behind people's backs. There's a tension working in rescue between having seen the worst of people and yet having to expect the best of them when you place a dog in their home. But a good rescue should treat you courteously, and although the process is involved, you get more in return out of it—a private rescue where dogs are living in a foster home can tell you more about the dog's behavior.

It's also important to be aware that while there are many great private rescues out there, in most places there's no official licensing procedure or government oversight of who can call themselves an animal rescue. So, the involved process also gives you a chance to judge the quality of the group you are working with. Ask questions back: What kind of behavior evaluations do they do? No dog is perfect, so are they honest about the issues? Are they providing routine care, such as flea and tick preventatives, and do they keep good medical records?

Keith also observes that a good rescue is one that does not take on more than it can handle, financially or expertise-wise. So, be careful of a rescue that thinks every dog can be saved, unless it somehow has basically infinite resources of time and money.

"We don't want to take a dog that needs rehabilitation that we can't offer," Keith says. "We have to have a foster home open and available that has the capability to give the dog what it needs." And the sad truth is that though there are many dogs with fixable problems that need rescue, there are some that for whatever reason are too far gone, and that is a reality that rescuers need to recognize. "We have had to turn down some beautiful dogs because of issues that we didn't think we could fix. We had to tell the shelter staff, this dog is never going to have a happy life."

Shelters

Shelters rarely have the resources for such a long process. You may not need to prove much more than that you own your home or have landlord permission to have pets. Even when there is more to the application than that, the process will be quicker—

many shelters even do same-day adoptions. The downside of the easy process is they will usually not know as much about the dog, so you may need to figure out if it's a good fit on your own. Here are some of the general types of experiences you can expect:

State-of-the-art shelters
If you're lucky, your local shelter is well-financed enough to be similar to a private rescue in what it can provide—medical care, behavioral evaluation, and enrichment and training for the dogs. A shelter like this will likely also have the resources to take the time to make good matches.

One shelter like this is Williamson County Animal Center in Tennessee. Director Laura Chavarria says their process involves a lot of individual conversation with potential adopters. "We talk to them about what they are looking for personality-wise, what they can handle, what would be a reason why they would bring the animals back—everyone has their limits. We understand that, and that's okay, but what would those limits be."

This conversation may steer you away from the dog you fell in love with at first sight—another part of the process where people may feel judged. But the shelter knows the dogs, and sometimes people need a reality check about whether, say, they can really raise a puppy when they're away from home 10 hours a day. In the long run it's for the benefit of both you and the dog. "We're doing this to make sure it's a good match—to save you heartbreak," she says. "Nobody wants to have that experience: 'Oh yeah, I adopted a dog from that shelter and it didn't work out; now I never want to adopt again.'"

Under-resourced shelters

In fact, remember you're lucky if you feel like you're being grilled, because that means the shelter has the resources to take that time and effort. The other extreme can be very different.

"There's a shelter in a neighboring county and they don't even have enough money to buy collars for all the dogs, so they can't even take them out and walk them every day," Chavarria says. "They don't have an adoption process. They just hand you a leash and tell you to take out any dog you want. If you want to adopt, you just come up and they literally just sign the adoption contract."

It's important to remember that the lack of resources is not a reflection on the dogs—there might be great dogs there. But it's a good idea to be aware of what you're going into in advance, because you still need to get a dog that is right for you for the rest of its life. "People make decisions based on emotion and that's not a good thing," Chavarria says. "Especially when you go into a shelter and see all these animals in cages and it seems like the staff doesn't care, you just want to take one home to save its life. But that might not be a good match."

And don't judge the people, either. No one dreams of growing up to run a terrible animal shelter, and the staff may be working hard to do the best they can in a difficult situation. Instead of blaming, get involved. "If go to your local shelter and you're not comfortable adopting, then there's a problem. Someone needs to get involved and show support."

What to Think About When Thinking About Adopting a Pit Bull

There are so many things to think about when you start looking for a dog that we could write a whole book just on that. Instead, here a few things that might be especially important if you're interested in adopting a pit bull type.

Breed characteristics

All dogs are individuals; you can't count on breed to predict everything about a dog. Still, if you get a pug and then complain that it snores, well . . . what did you expect? So, you need to be both aware of possible breed tendencies *and* make sure you get the individual that fits. Some dogs that look like pit bulls actually are purebred or purebred mixes, so remember the breed characteristics and think about how they might fit with what you want in a dog:

- **Some don't like other dogs or are selective about which individual dogs they'll tolerate.** It's okay for a dog not to like every other dog. (Do you like every other person?) But if your dream is to have a second dog, or you already have a dog, you need to choose carefully. This means you may need to steer clear of adopting a puppy, according to Heather Gutshall of Handsome Dan's Rescue in Rhode Island. "If you're adopting a dog to get along with another dog, it doesn't necessarily mean that by adopting a puppy you're going to get a dog that grows up to be dog social." No matter how a puppy is raised, some aspects of its temperament will only be possible to see once it has reached maturity. Puppies in general are sociable and tolerant of other dogs, so the fact that a puppy wants to play with every dog it sees is not a clue to what its adult temperament will be.

- **Remember that purebred pit bull breeds are high-energy dogs that need a job to do.** And maybe that's exactly what you want—maybe you want to do a dog sport or go on long hikes. For the wrong person, though, it can be a disaster. All the rescuers we talked to agreed that it's not hard to find a lower-energy pit bull type if you look—especially if you go for a mature dog. But make sure you pick the right individual with this in mind.

And one purely aesthetic consideration: If your attraction to the pit bull type is partly that you don't want a little foo-foo dog to dress in outfits, Heather Gutshall has a warning for you: "They

have short coats and no undercoats, so they're going to be cold, so make sure you're comfortable with your dog wearing a sweater."

Dogs with a past

Many pit bull rescues specialize in various types of rehabilitation, and have dogs they've taken from shelters or elsewhere for a variety of reasons. Some shelters still have a policy against adopting out pit bulls but can let them go to a private rescue. Some don't have the funds to treat medical issues. Some dogs have behavioral issues that make them difficult for a shelter to adopt out as is. Sometimes these are relatively trivial, such as dogs that are just jumpy and mouthy and need some basic manners training.

But some dogs do come from difficult backgrounds, and there are a lot of myths about them. Here are some things that rescues wish you knew:

- **Most fearful dogs were not abused, but undersocialized.** If a dog is afraid of men, say, people jump to the conclusion that the dog was mistreated by a man. "That's a huge misconception," says Gutshall, who specializes in fear and anxiety issues in dogs. "Only a small percentage of a time it's because the dog has actually been hurt by a human." Rather, it's likely that the dog wasn't exposed to enough men during the critical developmental period when it was a puppy.

- **Not every dog that has injuries was a "bait dog" or dogfighting dog.** "Any dog in a shelter with scars or wounds on him, the public wants to assume it was a bait dog," says Keith. "We try to make people understand that dogs are dogs, dogs have conflicts with other dogs—just because a dog has some wounds on him doesn't mean he was horribly abused or used for fighting. He could be a stray, got loose, met the wrong dog on the street. That's one of the biggest misconceptions."

- **It takes more than love to rehabilitate a fearful dog.** Most average dog owners wouldn't take on an aggressive dog. But they often think that for an extremely fearful dog, say from a hoarding or puppy mill situation, all it takes is love. Keith says it's very much the opposite. "A dog with clear-cut aggression, you know what they can and can't handle. The dogs that come from the hoarding cases where they're so mentally shut down, they're the ones that are the most unpredictable a lot of the time."

- **Dogs from a fighting background can make incredible pets.** Taking on a dog from a dogfight bust might seem like too much for the average owner. But Gutshall says there are groups that specialize in rescuing these dogs, and by the time they're up for adoption, they've been evaluated and rehabilitated by some of the best educated and experienced dog behaviorists in the country—not a process that you're likely to find happening in your local shelter.

While some of these dogs may be dog aggressive, this doesn't mean they're human aggressive, as these two traits are unconnected (and as we've mentioned earlier, in fact, human aggression was traditionally bred out of fighting dogs).

And living with these dogs can have special rewards. "Bringing a dog that has never been a pet into your home is really a beautiful thing. Helping them to see the joys of the world outside that life is really amazing and it's not really much different than adopting a shelter dog," says Gutshall. "I wouldn't rule those out for the average person. There are a lot of amazing dogs hidden away in dog-fighting yards."

Your Dog and the World

Another thing to consider when adopting a pit is that it will essentially always be onstage in a way that other breeds aren't. When your dog looks like a pit bull, if it lunges playfully at people, they're going to interpret it differently. It's not fair that some people will be more frightened than when, say, a Chihuahua lunges with actual aggression. But that's the reality: Your dog needs to be twice as good as other dogs for many people to think it's half as okay.

To have a dog who is comfortable enough in public to make a good impression, here are some things we think it's important to understand.

Know your dog's comfort level.

Most aggression is fear-based, and most animals fear what they're not familiar with. It's the safest way to react to an unpredictable world where an unfamiliar thing might be planning to eat you. But most people who see a lunging, barking pit bull don't think, "Oh, poor scared baby." So, it's your responsibility to do your best to make sure this doesn't happen. And that's not just for the benefit of all pit bulls—you also owe it to your dog, because why would you want to put your best friend through that kind of emotion?

Prevention is the best cure, says Drayton Michaels of Urban Dawgs, a trainer specializing in pit bulls, and a lot of times it's incredibly simple: "When your dog is uncomfortable, fearful, or stressed, or even overexcited, the best thing is to implement distance."

Know your own dog, and simply avoid situations that you know stress her out whenever you can. Do you already know that young kids or skateboards or other dogs make your dog react? Cross the street or turn around and go back the other way—going the long way round is better than putting both of you through the fear or overexcitement. And other people will thank you for it as well. "The dog haters and the dog lovers want the same thing," Michaels says. "Everybody wants a dog that's in the hands of capable people that's behaving appropriately."

Don't forget that it's your dog who gets to decide—even if you know there's no real threat, listen to your dog. That's whose judgment counts and you can't explain with words that she is safe. You may in fact need to protect her from people who love too much as well as who don't love—the person who runs up to your dog screaming that they love pit bulls, reaching out to grab her face and kiss it, probably seem scary from the dog's perspective, no matter how good their intentions are. Know how to say a polite no to people who want to pet your dog if you know she doesn't love it, or even if she normally does and but is in a particularly overstimulating or stressful situation where one more interaction might be too much.

To be your dog's advocate, you need to know she's uncomfortable, though, and many people aren't aware of the more subtle signals that a dog is stressed. Dogs are so tolerant that we often don't realize that they are only putting up with things they don't like—and because their body language differs from our own, we don't recognize we are pushing them and that they feel anxious or uncomfortable.

Most people recognize that a dog that's cowering is afraid, and if they're paying attention they may know that a tucked-in tail means that as well. But there are many other signals of stress in dogs that people either don't know or tend to misinterpret:

- Ears pinned back
- Wide eyes, or when you can see white around the side of the eye (what trainers call "whale eye")

- Yawning. This usually doesn't mean your dog is tired, but indicates stress.
- Lip lick when there's no food around
- Panting when it's not hot

Another thing to look out for is that thing dogs do where they shake their whole body as if they're wet, when they're not. The shake-off usually means they just experienced something they thought was a little bit hairy, but it went okay. "That can be a good indicator that they're processing stress well," Michaels says. But look back at what happened just before-hand and you'll learn something about how your dog feels about certain situations.

Growling, of course, is a sign that everyone understands, but owners often react to it inappropriately. It's particularly critical not to punish growling, since it's a signal that warns that a dog is being pushed to its limit. "The dog will learn not to growl or give you any kind of protracted warning sign, and that's when you get a dog that, quote-unquote, "bites out of nowhere,'" says Michaels.

It's also important to remember that behavior depends on context—what's okay in one situation may be too much to take in another, so just because your dog enjoys being petted, say, by familiar people at home, that doesn't guarantee she will enjoy it in public, or when the petters are strange young children.

Once you learn to recognize the physical signs of discomfort and stress, use them to make sure you don't push your dog beyond its comfort level. It's definitely possible to teach dogs not to fear things by counter-conditioning, but get a professional's help because it's a subtle and complicated process. Unlike puppies, who go through a developmental period where simple exposure teaches them not to fear, just throwing an adult dog in the deep end and exposing it to scary things will make matters worse.

And if you have a dog who is difficult in some situations, remember to be kind to both the dog and to yourself. Don't expect perfection: All you can do is do your best, stay flexible, and learn from each experience. "There's no hundred percent in behavior; you only get better percentages," says Michaels. "You can't predict what will happen in the environment, but you can prepare and respond in a better way."

Your dog and other dogs: on leash

If you have a pit bull who is not good with other dogs or only tolerates specific dogs that she knows, you probably already have the sense to avoid greeting other dogs on walks. You may be surprised to know though that most trainers think that on-leash greetings aren't a great idea, even if your dog is very dog-social.

Dogs have very specific rituals for polite greetings. "If you look at how dogs greet naturally, they don't greet nose to nose," says Michaels. What dogs want to do when they meet a stranger or acquaintance is sniff behinds, circle around, and maintain space to approach and retreat. All of these things are hard to do on a sidewalk, and being on leash makes it more difficult in more ways than one. "Dogs can't flee when on leash, so are already intrinsically a little stressed—even the best of dogs on leash may experience a little stress."

So, when we stop to meet another dog on a walk, we're asking them to greet head-on, which can actually be interpreted as hostile, when they're restrained in a way that adds stress to the situation. Often the humans are talking to each other and not paying attention to the subtle signals that the dogs are giving that they're uncomfortable. And if things don't go well, it's hard to retreat with your leashes all tangled. In most cases, it's just not worth it.

If an interaction does go badly it's not good either for your dog or for the reputation of pit bulls. Sometimes it takes only one scary encounter for your dog to develop a fear of all dogs. "Dogs generalize fear better than anything else," Michaels says. That's just dog nature—and it's human nature that people tend not to think their own dog is at fault. "Typically the person thinks it's the other dog's problem or fault." And perhaps even more so if your dog looks like a pit bull, so better not to risk playing into the stereotype. "If you have a dog that is already going to be pre-judged, you don't want to put them in a position where their reputation will be compromised."

Your dog and other dogs: off-leash play

Pit bulls sometimes like to play rough. So do Labs, but if a Lab knocks another dog down a little too hard, people tend to see it differently. You need to take the initiative to be aware of what is and isn't safe dog play and be even more careful than other people not to let it cross the line.

In recent years, off-leash dog parks have taken off all across the United States. You'd think dog trainers would be all in favor of this as an opportunity for dogs to exercise and socialize, but in fact, most think the risks outweigh the benefits. The problem is that properly supervising dog play is a job for an expert, whereas most owners seem to think no supervision is needed at all. On the contrary, you should be actively involved when your dog is playing with other dogs, even when it seems to be going fine.

"Dog play is largely founded in ritualized aggression," says Michaels. "Dogs are practicing their play moves and their fight moves and showing their weapons, but not going all the way and causing harm." So all that growling and chasing and pinning to the ground is in good fun—as long as the dogs are not overexcited, are taking turns, and are letting up before things get out of hand. But because they're using aggressive maneuvers, it's easy for play to tip over into a real fight—if someone's hurt by accident, if two dogs disagree on how hard is too hard, or if one dog is just kind of a pain in the butt and someone gets fed up.

So, when dogs are playing, the humans need to be involved to prevent that from happening. "I'm like an NBA referee—I'm up and down the court, I'm never more than three or four feet away from the dogs," says Michaels. And the referee isn't just pulling dogs out of the game for a break if they cross the line—he's keeping the play under control by intervening long before it gets to that point. You should be able to call your dog out of play on a regular basis, maybe ask for a simple cue like "touch," and then let her go back to the game. This helps keeps the arousal at a safe level so posturing and practicing the fight moves in play doesn't spill over into true aggression.

This need for active involvement for play to stay safe is one of the reasons many trainers recommend to their clients to avoid dog parks. Look around your local dog park. Are all the owners no more than three feet away from their dog? Can they call their dog out of the free-for-all once, let alone on a regular basis? Are they even paying attention, or are they drinking coffee and chatting with one another and looking at their phones?

And even if all the owners were supervising their dogs closely, another problem is that you don't know the history of all the dogs. Sadly, there are owners who will continue to bring their dog to parks despite repeated fights—maybe because they're jerks, but maybe just because of that natural human tendency to assume it's always some other dog's fault. And you will suffer the consequences even if your dog is an angel who

never starts a fight, because of the natural canine tendency to all join in the ruckus.

So, no matter how good your dog is socially, it's much safer for her to play with known dogs. Set up playdates with the dogs of friends or family. And even in those cases, you want to make sure they are dogs that play well with others. "Ask them these questions," Michaels recommends. "How many dog friends does your dog have? How often do they see them, and how well does play or greetings go? If the answers are lots of dogs, goes fine, never had any problems, those are the dogs you want to socialize your dog with. It's about a variety and abundance of social experiences that go well."

Communicating with your dog—positive versus negative

A dog that makes a good impression in public doesn't happen by accident. It happens when someone makes the effort to teach the dog good manners. Because this is so important for pit bulls, you're pretty much obligated to know more about training and behavior than most other dog owners do.

Don't think of training as a way to order your dog around. It's a way to communicate, and it works both ways. Your dog can learn that polite behavior makes good things happen for dogs. You can have a dog that does a quiet sit at your side when it's hoping really hard for one of your French fries, or one that paws at your arm till it hurts or barks till you get a headache. It's all the same to the dog, so why not choose the option that's more pleasant for you? And it is your choice, because it's all about how you react to and shape your dog's behavior.

Training is also only fair to your dog. Not knowing what's expected of it is stressful for any living creature. Imagine spending your whole life being randomly scolded for breaking rules you've never really been taught. Imagine not knowing what alternatives will keep you from being scolded. That's just as upsetting to a dog as it would be to you.

When you see training as a form of communication, positive reinforcement is the way to do the vast majority of it. Be wary of those who try to convince you differently because you have a large dog or an excitable one or one that is scary to other people. It helps a lot if you get into that argument to understand what positive reinforcement actually means. It's not "positive" in the sense of "everyone gets an award." It's not spoiling your dog by not having rules. It's a technical term, scientifically based. "Positive" in this context doesn't mean "nice"—in fact, there are such things as *positive punishment* and *negative reinforcement*. What *negative* and *positive* mean in this context is more like "subtracted" and "added." Positive reinforcement rewards the dog by adding something, such as a treat. Positive punishment also adds something, such as a collar jerk; in contrast, negative punishment removes something—such as pulling your hand away and refusing to play when a puppy nips.

Setting aside the technical terms, it's important to remember that training needs to tell a dog what it *can* do, not just what it can't. While you do need to be able to say no to your dog, most people way overuse the word and forget to give the dog alternatives. The dog can't just stand there frozen in one place all the time—it has to know what is okay to do instead of those things you inexplicably (to the dog) find annoying. So you need to be able to say yes to the dog as well, and that's what positive reinforcement does.

Once you think about being able to say yes to your dog, it can sometimes be more efficient. Let's face it, from the human point of view, there are a pretty limited set of natural dog behaviors that we actually want to live with. Positive reinforcement helps you say yes to the behaviors you like instead of having to say no to the almost infinite number of troublesome ideas that your dog can come up with. There are other techniques that work this way as well—think about, say, redirecting by taking away a shoe and giving your dog a chew toy. Saying yes to the chew toys instead of no to every single other object in the world is actually a lot less work. What these approaches have in common is focusing *your* attention on the behavior you want, instead of just the ones you don't like.

Effects of punishment on dog behavior

Again, we're not suggesting you never say no to your dog; your goal should be to clearly and calmly communicate both yes and

no. But when you're thinking about how to say no, it's important to be careful of the potential effects of positive punishment (which is what the rest of us mean when we say *punishment*). There's evidence that it can actually make behavior worse instead of better, even in areas that don't seem related to what you're training.

This has been demonstrated with punishment methods ranging from shock collars to yelling at the dog. Just ask dog owners—in fact, that's what a lot of the studies do. One presented a questionnaire to 364 owners, asking what training methods they used for some typical behaviors that most owners attempt to teach their pets, including "sit" and to come when called, and how good their dog's obedience was for those tasks. They found that the more the owners used punishment (mostly vocal punishment; only a minority used physical punishment), the worse the owner's own report of the dog's obedience was. Most respondents used a combination of reward and punishment. The minority who used only reward-based techniques showed the highest reported obedience; those using only punishment, the lowest.

The use of punishment also affected the dog's behavior in general, not just on the trained commands. The researchers asked about sixteen common behavioral problems and found that the number reported correlated with how much the owners used punishment-based training techniques. These behaviors included barking at dogs or people, aggression, fear, separation-related behaviors, and overexcitement. The greatest number of these problems was reported by owners using punishment only or a combination of punishment and reward—so basically, any amount of punishment caused a problem, even if positive reinforcement was also used.

Another study of dog owners found similar results about the influence of training methods on behavior aside from the trained behaviors. Owners who used positive reinforcement alone reported the fewest behavioral problems, including annoying attention-seeking behaviors, fear, aggression, and undesirable reactions to unfamiliar dogs and people.

One really interesting point comes out of a study of the behavioral problems associated with surrendering dogs to a shelter. Including all owners (both those relinquishing and a control group of people who kept their dogs), those who used choke and prong collars actually reported lower satisfaction with their dog's leash-walking behavior. So never mind the argument about whether they are humane or not—those collars just aren't doing the job.

More severe physical methods of punishment can actually cause behavioral problems, including aggression. One study found that a quarter of dogs responded aggressively to such techniques as being hit for undesirable behaviors, alpha rolls, and grabbing by the jowls and shaking. And who can blame them?

A good, skilled, science-based trainer should know how to use all four combinations of reward/punishment and positive/negative properly, and may be able to effectively include a limited role for positive punishment without bad effects. But these studies show what happens when the rest of us try it, so it's best to learn to do most of your communication with your dog in other ways.

Training with Shock

There's a good deal of controversy about shock collars in the training world. Some argue that electronic collars are safely used in sports such as field retrieving where dogs work at a great distance, and there are situations where it's argued that any risk they pose is worth it, such as rattlesnake avoidance training. However, shock collars are often recommended to average dog owners as well. Electronic fences are one example, and there are trainers whose business model involves training even simple obedience via e-collars.

So, it's worth being aware that training with shock has also been demonstrated to negatively affect a dog's behavior in general. One study of guard dog training compared shock collar training to training without it, and even though the non-shock training methods were fairly harsh, there was clear evidence of effects. Even when observed simply walking outside of training sessions, the shock-trained dogs showed behavior and body language evidence of stress, such as lowered ear position, which was not seen in the non-shock-trained dogs. There was also evidence that dogs developed a negative association with the actual training—in fact, one dog that yelped when given a shock in connection with a "heel" command, then yelped at the next "heel" without being shocked.

Electronic fence systems that use a shock collar have the same issues, and have been observed to sometimes cause aggression problems in previously non-aggressive dogs. Think about what it's like—imagine being shocked apparently randomly while walking around your yard and not really being able to understand why, since the overall concept of an invisible fence is beyond a dog's cognitive abilities. Not only is that at best bewildering, it sets the dog up to learn random associations with the shock. So, if a shock happens to be delivered when the dog sees something like another dog or a person, it can teach her to fear and react to those as well. (Also remember that an electronic fence doesn't keep other dogs and animals or people out of your yard and away from your dog.)

Punishment, Fear, and Reactivity

Despite all of this research and evidence, people with impressive-looking credentials may still try to sell you on harsh training methods. The owners of a young puppy recently told Deirdre that their veterinarian had advised them to sit on him, roll him, and "get in his face." And some "professional" trainers may try to convince you that shock training is the only approach to a severe behavioral problem, particularly aggression and reactivity.

They're correct that their methods will change the dog's behavior, but the cure is worse than the original problem. Shock basically works by teaching the dog to be afraid to act—it causes what psychologists call learned helplessness. So, it's a rather cruel approach to aggression and reactivity. Remember that those behaviors are caused by fear and anxiety. Do you really want to use a method that works by causing your dog additional fear and anxiety?

And this is true of any punishment-based approach to those issues. As we've already mentioned, punishing warning signs, such as growling, will just produce a dog that reacts "without warning"—because it doesn't change the way the dog feels, and eliminates any advance notice of her reaction. What's more, punishment increases arousal, which both interferes with learning, and pushes the animal closer to the threshold for reaction and aggression. And there's also just simple cause and effect: You see a dog coming and jerk your dog's leash. Your dog sees the dog that's approaching and associates it with the pain or discomfort of the collar jerk. So, the next time it sees a dog, it expects that unpleasant thing to happen again. No wonder the dog's behavior when it sees another dog gets worse and worse. Rather than using methods that teach dogs additional fear in the face of what they fear, a skilled, science-based trainer can use counter-conditioning to gradually build up a positive emotional association instead.

CHAPTER 5

your dog and
the law

Having a pit bull as a family dog is usually delightful, but it can also be stressful, despite the fact that your dog is no different than any other. The challenges faced by the average dog owner pale in comparison to what some pit bull owners go through. In this chapter we'll help you understand the state of laws specifically directed at pit bulls and what to do if you are affected. Rest assured, we are not trying to dissuade anyone from having a pit bull dog as a pet. It is our hope to have such dog owners as educated ambassadors as well!

A Dog by Any Other Name

Breed-discriminatory laws, otherwise known as breed-specific legislation (BSL), are laws set up to regulate dogs based on their look rather than by their actions or behavior. The pit bull-type dog was not the first dog in the United States to face such a ban. Long Branch, New Jersey, residents banned the Spitz in 1878. Just a few years after that, bloodhounds were banned in Massachusetts. Later, at the height of the pit bull panic in the 1980s, communities began to introduce breed bans with the intent of reducing or halting a perceived dog bite epidemic.

Thankfully BSL is starting to find its way out of most law books. The trouble with this type of legislation begins with the notion that regardless of breed, all dogs have teeth and can bite, and that law-abiding citizens, who are not the target of such legislation, are the people most affected by these laws. Negligent owners are the least likely to abide by new rules, whereas responsible dog owners are being forced to give up their dogs because of the negligent few.

In this chapter, we will take a look at some cities, states, and even countries that have had blanket laws targeting pit bulls. We will see what initiated such laws and then, similarly, what is replacing them. As the evidence will show, BSL has killed many innocent family dogs without reducing dog bites.

Across the Sea

The Netherlands sought to increase public safety by putting a breed ban in place in 1993, when a child lost its life to a dog attack. After keeping its breed ban in place for 15 years, however, the Dutch government saw that dog bites increased after the ban went into place. They realized that they were wasting resources. So, in 2008, the legislators repealed their ban and focused on behavior rather than looks. The country now focuses on enforcing leash laws and dedicates resources to owner education programs.

When targeting dogs based on looks and alleged breed, the trouble is that you are creating a false sense of safety. You are also expending energy and resources on rounding up so-called dangerous dogs that were not the problem to begin with. Let's look at another example. The Dangerous Dog Act of 2000 in Aragon, Spain, placed severe restrictions on dog owners. Multiple dog breeds including rottweilers, Dobermans, and pit bull-type dogs were blacklisted. If a person wanted to keep one of these dogs as a companion, the dog would have to be muzzled at all times while on leash. Dogs and their owners are also required to undergo psychological testing.

According to a study published in the *Journal of Veterinary Behavior* in 2007, popular breeds, such as the German shepherd and crossbreed dogs, accounted for the great majority of the incidents during the two periods of study. Specifically, the German shepherd proved to be overrepresented significantly among the canine population. Dogs on the dangerous breeds list, on the other hand, were involved in a small proportion of the incidents both before and after the introduction of legislation.

Italy gave up its breed-specific legislation and traded it in for breed-neutral laws. Scotland also did away with BSL, but until the United Kingdom follows suit, it does not have full control until the Dangerous Dog Act (DDA) eliminates its breed-specific language. The dog bite trends in the UK are alarming and have increased tremendously since the enactment of the DDA and low-income areas seem to be the most affected, according to a report from the Health and Social Care Information Center in the UK. In the mid-1990s, the Dangerous Dog Act was evaluated by the UK to see if it had achieved success in reducing dog bites. What do you think was discovered in the findings? You guessed it! No effect on reducing bites, since there weren't any resources dedicated to ways to actually lower the incidence of dog bites (such as reduced tethering, the use of leashes, and not allowing dogs to run at large). An interesting tidbit discovered by the Aberdeen Royal Infirmary was that "human bites were as common as those from the most implicated dog breed."

Many professional organizations in the UK, including the

British Veterinary Association, Blue Cross, the Kennel Club, RSPCA, and Dogs Trust, are speaking against breed-specific legislation. Some reports show that the UK has spent millions of dollars enforcing a ban that is doing nothing to educate the public about proper bite prevention.

In the United States

Let's review what is happening in some US cities that are maintaining their breed-specific legislation, before we get to the somewhat happy ending. In Prince George's County, Maryland, a ban was initiated in 1996. This is a region with nearly 10 percent of its citizens living below the poverty line. Its animal control officers are working around the clock to answer complaint calls about the presence of pit bulls. Recently, a local family was saved by their dog who alerted them about their house fire, but when the responders arrived and saw that the dog that saved them was a pit bull type, they alerted animal control and the dog was seized, even after this heroic act. The family had to give her up.

This is the kind of unnecessary tragedy facing families in BSL jurisdictions. In Omaha, Nebraska, multiple purebred dogs are considered to be "pit bulls" and thus must be muzzled if they fall under the ridiculous definition of "pit bull," which is: "any dog that is an American pit bull terrier, American Staf-

fordshire terrier, Staffordshire bull terrier, Dogo Argentina, Presa Canario, Cane Corso, American bulldog, or any dog displaying the majority of physical traits of any one or more of the above breeds (more so than any other breed), or any dog exhibiting those distinguishing characteristics which substantially conform to the standards established by the American Kennel Club or United Kennel Club for any of the above breeds." It gets worse. The city's humane society is awarded $100,000 annually to maintain the breed restrictions and to enforce citations for violating this mandate. Bite rates have only increased since the inception of this mandate and naturally, the most popular breeds are often the ones cited for the most bites in a region. The main biters in 2012 were the Labrador retriever, not because this breed is more aggressive, but because they're the most common. They also do not fall under the muzzle requirement under this act. Negligent owners are not held accountable unless they have one of the dog breeds or mixes deemed problematic in Omaha.

BSL Done and Undone

While some jurisdictions are considering new BSL, many places are doing away with it. South Hutchinson, Kansas, traded in its twenty-two-year ban during a periodic review of its ordinance book. The city realized that since it already had a vicious dog ordinance that would deal with nuisance dogs, it did not need to also single out specific breeds. The lifting of this ban will help unburden the local shelter and will help healthy, adoptable dogs of all kinds find their forever homes. The Kansas suburb of Roeland Park repealed a twenty-seven-year-old ban on pit bulls and eliminated breed-specific legislation in favor of a better definition of nuisance animals, which includes a definition of "vicious animals" and even includes language on tethering (chaining) dogs. Nine cities in Missouri lifted breed bans between 2011 and 2014; most of these bans were over 20 years old.

The town of Moreauville, Louisiana, had voted to enact a ban on pit bulls and rottweilers, but after much public pressure, including television interviews with a family being affected by the ban, the town decided against it. Deirdre even called the local government to request that it reconsider its stance and the clerk she spoke to urged her to tell everyone that had been calling, that the town decided against the ban. The collective energy of the story of a family that was about to be torn apart by BSL, especially when it was going to affect a little girl with medical problems, helped turn this near ban into a no-go. This is why we urge citizens to monitor their own communities and to get active so that, if matters like this arise, they can be addressed before a ban is ever initiated.

South Dakota and Utah became the eighteenth and nineteenth states to prohibit breed-specific provisions. Utah's Senator Weiler noted, in a video against BSL, that seizures of family dogs, criminal charges, and fines were taking place with citizens simply walking with their dogs when crossing city borders where there weren't restrictions and crossing into cities that had restrictions. Senator Dayton of Utah addressed the issue from the stance of property rights and appealed to conservatives that believe that dog owners have the right to choose. In South Dakota, a "Find the Pit Bull" slideshow was presented to lawmakers, and the lawmakers addressed the issue that dangerous dogs are the result of negligent and reckless dog owners, not the dogs themselves.

Ohio was the only state to enact breed-specific legislation back in the 1980s but finally elected to lift it in 2012, via House Bill 14. While the bill allowed individual communities to maintain any breed-specific language, the state itself no longer defines pit bulls as being "vicious," "dangerous," or "nuisance" dogs, but instead maintains breed neutrality in its animal laws.

A multitude of cities and states are trading in these archaic laws for more effective community-centric, breed-neutral laws. To date, as this book is being published, there are nineteen states that prohibit BSL. Two of those states, Colorado and Florida, have some of the worst breed-prohibitive cities in the United States today. In Colorado, Denver, and Aurora continue to hold on to their breed bans despite expensive lawsuits paid for by taxpaying citizens, and despite their bite statistics rising instead of falling. Aurora considered lifting its breed ban, but the proposal was overturned after a public vote took place. Some believe that this happened because voters have no experience with banned breeds and therefore, have no real stake in lifting the ban, but also because local press presented skewed data that made it seem as if Aurora would be better off without the banned breeds in its jurisdiction. When Deirdre was recently speaking about BSL at a pet expo where pit bulls are banned, she was pulled aside by an area police officer who confided that he is personally against the ban and that he did not become a police officer to round up family dogs. He even said that when we comes across pit bulls from time to time, he takes them home and finds rescues that can help get them out of city limits to safety. According to a 2014 article in *USA Today*, more than 100 municipalities have overturned bans and restrictions against pit bulls and mixed-breed dogs that look like them. In a meeting about a breed-specific proposal, the police chief in Wooster, Ohio, spoke against his city's breed ban when he noted that his department is not equipped to enforce the ban: "Officers aren't trained for that." He explained the police would need to transport dogs in their cruisers for DNA tests, in order to properly identify them, "And if an owner says no, then we need to go to a judge for a search warrant." After the meeting, the council approved a breed-neutral dangerous dog ordinance.

Breed-Specific Legislation and Your Dog

While breed-discriminatory laws and policies do still exist in many places, many of us have experienced it firsthand in other ways, such as when we travel with our pets or try to rent housing. There are many nuances to the law that all dog owners should be aware of, even if they don't have a targeted dog. We don't intend to scare you away from choosing to keep a pit bull for a pet, but to help you maintain your commitment to being your dog's best advocate and to help you understand how to keep it away from the law and in your loving home.

If you do not have a pit bull-type dog or other type of dog affected by BSL, you may have never heard of such a thing and probably find it fairly alarming! Deirdre talks to people about breed bans nearly every day, often people in her audience at expos have never heard of BSL or cannot believe that a dog could be taken from its owners if they, for example, travel with it through Denver, Colorado. A few online maps listing US cities with breed bans have been created to help people know whether they are traveling through or moving to a city with such a ban. It is important to be informed, not just for your own sanity and to avoid lawsuits, but to protect your dog from this known and very dangerous bias. At the end of the day, owners are the people culpable for the behavior and actions of their dog. Although a dog may be sentenced to death for his actions, owners have to live with the consequence of their action or inaction on behalf of their dog.

How will you protect yourself and your dog against this issue, then?

- Know whether you are moving to or traveling through an area that has a breed ban.
- If you have never DNA-tested your dog, chances are you or a pet professional has guessed what breed type your dog is and marked it on his vet records. Go back to your vet and ask that your dog be listed instead as a shelter mix or mixed-breed dog, since you genuinely do not know what your dog is mixed with.
- If you live in a town with a breed ban and cannot move, it is best to steer clear from calling your dog a pit bull, even on such places as social media.
- If you are asked by animal control to name the breed of your dog or the percentage of breed(s) in your dog, unless you have registration of purebred status, do not play along. You have a mixed-breed dog.
- Know the law in your city. Know what your police and animal control officers have the right to do and what they do not have the right to do.

- Get involved in your local community, especially city council meetings. Become a friendly and familiar face that actively participates in what is happening in your town. It could be the exact thing that keeps your dog out of harm's way. Do this not just to safeguard your family from breed bias, but because it is important to care about where you live.

Fighting Back: What to Ask For Instead of BSL

Outlawing a dog based on how it looks will not keep us safe from a dog bite. What will keep us safe, on the other hand, is introducing breed-neutral laws for all dog owners to comply with. We recommend the following:

- Ask lawmakers for breed-neutral dangerous-dog legislation. This allows animal control to enforce true dangerous-dog issues without having to drive around speculating about whether a dog is a pit bull.
- Ask lawmakers to support education efforts to ensure that parents are aware of the whereabouts of their children and the way that children interact with dogs.
- Ban chaining/tethering or at the very least, require dog owners to be present when their dog is tethered.

- Do not allow at-large dogs to roam. Enact leash laws if there are not already leash laws.

- Penalize the people that are noncompliant and elevate fines for repeat offenders. Fines can help increase funding for educational materials.

- Encourage breed-neutral spay-and-neuter programs, and when possible, offer those programs at low or no cost to low-income dog owners.

- Encourage the licensing of breeding, though this can be challenging, since backyard breeders are not necessarily going to comply without the risk of fines and enforcement.

- Require licensing and necessary vaccinations, such as rabies shots. This is obvious, but many dog owners are not in compliance with licensing. This might be due a fear of breed-specific bans, ignorance, or general outlaw behavior.

- Teach dog bite prevention to dog owners and non-dog owners.

- Make whistleblowing options available to people aware of dogfighting activity in their community; for example, a toll-free phone number.

- Note that breed bans are a violation of property rights.

- Point out to lawmakers that BSL is expensive for taxpayers and sends the wrong message to responsible dog owners when they are being singled out. There's a great BSL calculator available online at bestfriends.guerillaeconomics.net. Make lawmakers aware that that BSL does not reduce dog bites.

Essentially, dog bite prevention policy should focus on the factors that we see again and again in dog bite incidents. Ohio was one of the first to pass a breed ban. This statewide ban was a result of multiple dog attacks that took place in the late 1970s and early 1980s. Dog-related incidents seemed to be on the rise in the 1970s through mid-1980s, prior to the enactment of breed-specific bans against pit bulls, but also prior to the enactment of leash laws in most jurisdictions. Well-meaning government officials sought to protect their citizens from what seemed like a breed-specific problem, but on closer examination, a common theme in these incidents centered around at-large (unleashed) roaming dogs and dogs living in yards, often unaltered and unsupervised. The chase instinct of free-roaming dogs was stimulated when they encountered people. Chained dogs likewise reacted to the appearance of people or other animals on "their" turf.

Rather than evaluating these common threads and monitoring these problem dog owners, the state took a sweeping stance against what they believed to be a pit bull problem. When a dog lives on a chain for most of its life, it causes serious behavioral issues; as observed in *A Lawyer's Guide to Dangerous Dog Issues*, "There is ample evidence that chaining causes psychological, emotional, and behavioral problems in dogs. It ruins the dogs' nature as social pack animals . . .

How to Protect Yourself from a Dog

Now is as good a time as any to help illustrate how to react if you think an at-large dog is following you. We want to see a reduction in dog bites on a global scale and this information, provided, by the Humane Society of the United States (HSUS), could help in that reduction:

- Resist the impulse to scream and run away.
- Remain motionless, hands at your sides, and avoid eye contact with the dog.
- Once the dog loses interest in you, slowly back away until he is out of sight.

- If the dog does attack, "feed" him your jacket, purse, bicycle or anything that you can put between yourself and the dog.
- If you fall or are knocked to the ground, curl into a ball with your hands over your ears and remain motionless. Try not to scream or roll around.

We would add that you should also instruct children not to run or scream, as challenging as that may be for them, it could save them from a great deal of hurt and pain. Many educators refer to the concept of "being like a tree."

Media reports on dog attacks often portray the dog as a "family pet" that one day "inexplicably became dangerous—but a dog living on the end of a chain 24 hours a day is not a family pet, and the temperament of a dog that has been chained incessantly is quite EXPLICABLE."

Chained dogs were regularly the subjects of these dog bite incidents, but the general way of addressing the issue of dog bites was never to address chaining. This is baffling, knowing that we could have prevented a great number of dog attacks thirty-plus

years ago. The National Canine Research Council (NCRC) high-lights an important distinction, which helps shape our under-standing of these unnecessary bite incidents:

- A RESIDENT DOG: Resident dogs are dogs, whether confined within a dwelling or otherwise, whose owners maintain them in ways that isolate them from regular, positive human interactions. The isolation and lack of exposure to the family unit results in the display of behaviors different from Family dogs.
- A FAMILY DOG: Family dogs are dogs whose owners keep them in or near the home and also integrate them into the family unit, so that the dogs learn appropriate behavior through interaction with humans on a regular basis in positive and humane ways.

This distinction is important whenever you find a dog bite story in the news. Often, the author will refer to the dog as a "family dog" when in fact that dog lives outside, often without shade, food, or guidance. That, dear reader, is a resident dog and can one day become a bite risk, or already has. This is by no means the fault of the dog. In the right care, that dog still has a chance of becoming a family dog.

Unintended Adverse Effects of BSL

Proponents of breed bans, in their shortsighted goals to eradicate pit bull-type dogs do not think as much about the adverse effects of a breed ban. If we are banning dogs because we fear irresponsible dog owners, we have to think about the kind of outlaws that live without honoring basic societal rules. Instead, we are punishing the people that are not the problem while expecting those that live outside of the law to suddenly conform to it. This makes little sense.

Another unintended effect could be that many people who love their dog, and are not in the position to move if BSL is suddenly enforced, may choose to hide their dog and possibly stop taking him to the vet, for fear of having their beloved pet taken away. Imagine the impact it would have on public health and welfare if people stopped getting their dogs vaccinated against rabies, for example. Add to that the effects on the mental health of a dog that, hidden away, is no longer able to get adequate exercise or walks on leash. This could have dire consequences for the dog, his owner, and their community. This is not what BSL intends, but it is certainly a by-product.

Outlaws will not become law-abiding citizens just because a ban is initiated. In fact, many outlaws will seek out banned breeds for status symbols or will just choose another dog with a similar build.

States That Prohibit BSL

The following states prohibit their municipalities from passing breed-specific laws: Colorado, Connecticut, Florida, Illinois, Maine, Massachusetts, Minnesota, New Jersey, Nevada, New York, Ohio, Oklahoma, Pennsylvania, Rhode Island, South Dakota, Texas, Utah, and Virginia.

One state, California prohibits most breed-specific laws, but allows breed-specific spaying/neutering.

Do We Want Dangerous Dog Laws?

Yes! We want to ensure the safety of the people and animals that we love. It is important to remember that it is a privilege to own a dog, not a fundamental right. We never want to set a dog up to fail. If we know, for example, if our dog does not like men in uniform, we can certainly work with a trainer to work that out. But in the meantime, we can also protect the animal from encountering that experience if we are not comfortable with that interaction. That is perfectly okay, and we would encourage thinking of your dog and the potential challenge when you make that choice.

Deirdre has a dog named Baxter Bean who she knows can be fearful of large crowds. When he was younger, she worked with him to try to change that experience to a more positive one. However, over the years, she has come to understand that he may never be great in a crowd. Thus, she does not set him up to fail—

rather she shelters him from that experience. Baxter Bean came to Deirdre in his fifth month of life, clearly having already experienced trauma, since he is covered in chemical- or fire-caused scarring from his neck down to his thighs. Although she will never know exactly what happened to cause his fears, she knows his limits and works to create new positive experiences that he can enjoy and grow through.

What Does Having BSL Teach Our Children?

We do not want our children to experience the loss of a beloved pet because of discrimination. Nor do we want them to learn to fear authority. We want to encourage the joy of the human-canine bond with our children and by doing so, help them to become compassionate, responsible, and caring people. BSL can deeply affect a child and shape who he or she becomes as an adult. So, it is important, not only for dogs but for our next generation of humans, that adults with the voice to change such legislation speak out against this practice.

Other Breed-Specific Issues

Perhaps you live in a city that does not have a breed ban, but you have just decided to purchase a house and need home-

The American Bar Association Position Statement on BSL

American Bar Association (ABA) House of Delegates Resolution 100-2012:

RESOLVED, That the American Bar Association urges all state, territorial, and local legislative bodies and governmental agencies to adopt comprehensive breed-neutral dangerous dog/reckless owner laws that ensure due process protections for owners, encourage responsible pet ownership and focus on the behavior of both dog owners and dogs, and to repeal any breed-discriminatory or breed-specific provisions.

owners' insurance. You call your local insurance rep and find out, to your disbelief, that your insurance company will not insure your home because you have a dog that has made its "do not insure" list. Do not despair. Many insurance companies, such as State Farm, are actively breed-neutral. Many advocacy groups, such as Pinups for Pitbulls, Inc., keep lists on their website so that you can easily find what you need without having to do a lot of legwork. Some states, such as Pennsylvania, even ban breed restrictions by insurance companies. There is a great deal of lobbying around this issue each year and hopefully more insurance companies will change their language to reflect breed-neutral positions.

Alternatively, imagine you need to rent an apartment. When beginning your search, you start to see discriminatory

The Dangers of Encouraging Any Breed-Specific Policy

Some policies that single out pit bulls are supposedly meant to protect them. For example, some shelters have extra requirements for adopting a pit bull, above and beyond assuring that they're permitted where the adopter resides. One prominent example of a group advocating for special policies is PETA, which supports what it calls "breed-specific protection" for pit bulls, in the form of legal requirements that pit bull dogs be spayed or neutered.

Why single out pit bulls? PETA argues:

In fact, PETA advocates for a ban on breeding all dogs, including pit bulls as breeding any dogs should be illegal as long as millions must be euthanized in animal shelters every year. But more than any other breed, pit bulls are in crisis and need help right now. They face systemic, relentless abuse and neglect. They are also the most frequently abandoned dog breed, and as a result, tens of thousands of pit bulls must be euthanized in shelters every year. . . . Requiring that they be spayed or neutered means that fewer will be born into abusive, neglectful homes—it's that simple.

But is it that simple? Spaying and neutering of all adoptable animals is standard practice in the shelter and rescue community. Efforts to encourage owners to spay and neuter their pets has been one of the most successful initiatives of humane groups in recent decades. So there's no need to single out pit bulls, and the danger of doing so is that it has the effect of making pit bulls seem different—exactly what we are arguing against in this book.

In this context, it's worth pointing out that you should always think about the bigger agenda of any group or authority that's recommending a policy. You may be surprised to know that in PETA's ideal world, no one would have a pit bull—or any other dog, because no one would have pets:

We at PETA very much love the animal companions who share our homes, but we believe that it would have been in the animals' best interests if the institution of "pet keeping"—i.e., breeding animals to be kept and regarded as "pets"—never existed.

Some Professional Organizations That Oppose BSL

American Bar Association (ABA)

American Kennel Club (AKC)

American Veterinary Medical Association (AVMA)

American Society for the Prevention of Cruelty to Animals (ASPCA)

Association of Pet Dog Trainers (APDT)

Centers for Disease Control and Prevention (CDC)

National Animal Control Association (NACA)

The Obama administration even spoke out against BSL, stating, "We don't support breed-specific legislation—research shows that bans on certain types of dogs are largely ineffective and often a waste of public resources."

language such as "no pit bulls, rottweilers, etc." What do you do? Do you get a DNA test that will indicate your dog is not on the list of undesirables? Is your dog a purebred with papers? You can go that route in challenging matters, but we would also like to point out some other options. First, you can ask your potential landlords to meet your dog to show that you are a responsible owner with a well-behaved dog. Second, you can ask them to be clear about their concerns. They themselves might not want to be discriminatory, but their insurance company might be. Third, do not give up. Some people give up easily and will surrender their dog to a shelter. Remember that you chose to include this dog in your family. There are organizations that offer all kinds of resources, such as temporary foster homes, and websites devoted to dog-friendly, breed-neutral housing.

Become a resource in your community for city council, for your neighbors, and most of all, for your family dog. A well-versed advocate in the community can be instrumental to keeping BSL from rising up or in squashing it as fast as it is introduced. Deirdre lived in Pennsylvania with her first pit bull, Carla Lou. When a neighboring town tried to enact a breed-specific muzzle law against pit bulls, she found herself having to call the city's lawyers to educate them about the rules in their own state. You can do this, too. You might have to one day. Your dog will be well protected when you are calm, assertive, and armed with the facts. Your dog should get to live out her life with you.

CHAPTER 6

how to talk to people about pit bulls

D eirdre works in dog advocacy in her daily life as the CEO of Pinups for Pitbulls, Inc. (PFPB). Each day, she is presented with new challenges about how to speak about dogs to people. She receives calls from people who want to interview her, people who need to rehome a dog, and occasionally, people who think that she is the reason that dog attacks occur in their community. It can be an interesting dance between so many emotional topics and she knows that if she missteps, it can have grave consequences for dogs known as pit bulls.

In developing this chapter, we imagined various scenarios that are common for not just dog advocates but people who are simply walking their dog down the street. How do you effectively deal with someone shouting to "get that damn pit bull off my street?" What should you do when your local news outlet presents inaccurate information about pit bulls? Here's our advice on how to approach these and other scenarios.

Listen First, Even to People Who Have Opposing Views

The most important thing is to always listen first, and be open to those who aren't dog people in the same way that you are. With this patient and thoughtful approach, Deirdre and her organization have had groundbreaking moments at their informational booths in places where people might be "unconverted" or ignorant about dog advocacy: tattoo conventions, comic book conventions, and music festivals. New relationships have been fostered among so many different walks of life. We have talked about dogs to Irish-born military servicemembers whose hobbies are training IED detection dogs, including their own pit bull-type dog. We have talked with uniformed officers, politicians, young children, elderly men and women, statistics professors, and general dog lovers. When we talk to people, we remain open to hearing their perspective, their story, and their beliefs. We patiently await an opening in the conversation to educate, as needed, or to simply just enjoy hearing what they have to offer. We learn, too!

"My dog was attacked by my neighbor's pit bull."

Here's an example of what can happen when you listen first and then think of how to respond before you condemn a point of view that's different from yours. While she was standing in the booth at a tattoo convention, an older gentleman walked up to Deirdre and began ranting about how his dog was attacked by his neighbor's pit bull. She asked him in a calm manner to tell her exactly what happened. She let him know she was there to listen. He appeared to be somewhat surprised that she did not argue with him. He went on to tell her that his small bichon got loose and ran into his neighbor's yard where a pit bull was kept chained to a tree without food or shade. Deirdre nodded. He said the pit bull tried to grab his dog but the bichon slipped loose. Since the neighbor's dog was chained, he was lucky enough to get his dog back, safe from harm. She asked him if his dog lived inside. He said, "Of course." She then asked if his dog had access to food and water. Again, he exclaimed, "Of course!" He began to see where she was going with this.

"It's interesting to see that your own dog has care, food, water, and shelter but this neighbor dog seemed like a nuisance because of his alleged breed and circumstance, rather than your seeing your neighbor as the problem," Deirdre finally said, politely. He said that he hadn't thought of it that way. He had just assumed these were problem dogs, instead of thinking of people treating dogs in this way as being problem owners.

"Pit bulls can be companion dogs?!"

It's also important to remember that some people are simply uninformed. An exchange at one tattoo convention at a four-star hotel in Asheville, North Carolina, was especially eye-opening. People were able to walk through the vendor halls even if they were not there for the convention itself. An elderly woman read

the words "companion animals" in the PFPB mission statement on its banner. She had no idea pit bulls could be pets. She had only ever heard of them as fighting dogs. She was very excited and could not wait to tell others what she learned. You just never know what will happen when you leave your comfort zone.

All Dogs Are Special

When you're done listening and it's your turn to talk, consider talking about pit bulls as they are: dogs. They are all individual dogs, with history for some and unknown origins for others. Let's talk about them from what we know to be true and skip speculating beyond what we know. Not every shy dog was abused, and not every dog with scars was involved in dogfighting. Deirdre's very own pit bull mix, Carla Lou, was beaten up by the three cats that she lived with. Her scars could have been interpreted as dogfight scars, but really, she just lived with some strong-willed cats!

As dogs, they're special to their owners—and this is just like any other breed. Consider thinking about it this way: To the collie enthusiast down the street, you might seem aggressively passionate about your favorite dog. No judgment, but imagine the day that you might need to find some support, should you ever find yourself in front of a city council meeting trying to explain that these dogs are individuals, and that they deserve a fair shake. In other words, have all of the pit bull pride in the world, but remain open. You might need other dog-loving allies and they might be hard to find if you maintain a separatist attitude in your approach.

"Punish the Deed, Not the Breed"

Pinups for Pitbulls used to use the slogan "Punish the Deed, Not the Breed" until PFPB evaluated the confusion that such a

slogan might create. Does that statement foster conversation or just add questions?

When you wear this slogan, are you prepared to explain how this happens? If so, excellent! Arm yourself with facts and engage people openly in conversation. Since PFPB reevaluated its slogan, it was changed to "Take My Leash, Not My Life"™, which more directly asks people to think about the effect that being a responsible dog owner can have by obeying leash laws and leading positively. A lack of responsibility on the dog owners' part can lead to a fatal ending. Deirdre has seen people read this slogan and cry. We need to build relationships, build alliances, and foster relationships to bring about change for the long run. We can do this through positive and inclusive messaging.

Present a Positive Face

When you're walking your dog, here's some ways to help change perception on behalf of pit bulls. Please read this list with an open heart and try not to read it as dictatorial, for it is simply meant to help all dogs get a positive reaction:

- Hold your head up, smile, and engage people around you. Say hello!
- If your dog likes to doll up, add a bow tie or flower to her collar.

Deirdre's dog Baxter Bean wears the kind of head halter used to stop leash pulling, which looks to some people like a muzzle. She has him wear one in hot pink. You would be amazed at the confusion on people's faces when they first see him in it. A 65-pound male pit bull in what appears to be a muzzle but is hot pink. It's comical! Some people will ask if it's a muzzle and she will explain that it is not. He has full range of motion for his head and his mouth can still drink water and accept treats. People are still often cautious but it fostered conversation, which is a plus!

- If people shout at you about having "that dog" on the same street as them, you can take multiple approaches depending on the scene:

  a. Pretend that you didn't hear them and keep walking. It hurts, we know, but when people are that ignorant, it is not always the best time to try to educate them.

  b. Take a snapshot in your mind of what they look like. If you choose not to engage this time, when you see them next time, give them a pamphlet or a fact sheet containing information about pit bull dogs. Tell them that you would love to talk to them sometime and, if they are open to it, ask them to meet your dog (assuming your dog is comfortable meeting new people).

  c. Shout back, "Have a great day!" This sounds a little passive-aggressive but it doesn't have to be. Or even, "Thank you."

Confuse them; maybe they don't think you heard them right.

What is most important is that you maintain your calm and do not return hostility with hostility. It is tempting, yes, but your dog is unable to speak up for herself. She relies on you to be a good representative. It does not help your dog's reputation when you act out in anger.

Go home and gripe about that jerk on a dog forum, but making a negative scene or engaging in such individuals' negative worldview does not help the cause. Take a deep breath, look into your dog's eyes, and breathe again. You are your dog's voice, be her best voice.

Educate Against the Hate

You just read today's headline and it irrationally damns pit bulls. This is your chance to educate the author. If you call the media source screaming or scream in the comments section of an online article, do you think the author or editor will listen? Do you listen when someone yells at you and tells you that you are wrong? Probably not.

What should you do then? First, find what was not factual in the article and look up the actual data that proves the article wrong. Send a letter to the editor, saying that you would like a

The Media Are People, Too

When a news article includes information that you know is incorrect, you don't have to lie down and take it. But before you react, always think about the person on the other side of the conversation.

Reporters don't go into the news business because they love the thrill of spreading misinformation. They are no doubt overworked and somewhat burnt out, given the state of the industry these days, but they are there because they're curious about the world and enjoy digging to get at the truth. And remember they've potentially got the ear (or eye) of a large number of people. You want to win them over to your side, and you're not going to do that by accusing them of being malicious, deliberate liars, or idiots.

So, approach your communications with writers as an opportunity for education. Most reporters covering a dog bite story have no background in anything relating to animals. There's no reason they would know to doubt when a police source tells them a dog is a pit bull, until you explain why they should.

When you contact a reporter, remember they are busy people who may have half a dozen stories to write immediately and not a lot of time to think about the one they wrote yesterday that you're so angry about. Keep it short, give them something to think about, and offer references or your own availability to talk for the rest. Provide corrections in a way that assumes you're talking to an intelligent person who can think for himself or herself. Good reporters like to dig down and expose lies and misinformation, so a couple of well-chosen tidbits that pique curiosity will be more effective than a diatribe of several pages that gets deleted unread.

At the end of your message (which you've spell-checked, and ideally allowed a reliable friend to look over), include all of your contact information and offer your help for the future: as a source if you're in a position to speak as an authority, to connect the writer with reliable experts if you're not, or as a voice for another side of the story in the future. A big part of a reporter's job is finding trustworthy sources and if writers think you can save them time doing this, they may very well take you up on it.

This kind of approach has worked for Deirdre time and again. The very first time she contacted a reporter, she was openly upset about the way that a prominent cover story was presented but also remained respectful and requested that he contact her if he ever wanted to present a different perspective on pit bull stories. He wrote her back immediately and requested a call. It turned out that they shared a love of large-breed dogs and he offered Deirdre the chance to be quoted in the follow-up piece. Ask and you shall receive! He then offered her a page 3 spot highlighting the efforts of Pinups for Pitbulls, Inc. They still follow each other's work to this day.

In her experience, asking goes a long way while remaining calm, firm, but fair.

Also, don't forget: Don't write only when you're angry! If you read an article that gets it right, its author deserves positive reinforcement. Reporters get notes of praise so infrequently that they make a big impression. Don't forget to offer your assistance on future stories with a message like this one as well, since you're making contact with someone who went the extra mile to get it right. They deserve your help, too.

Finally, remember that reporters rarely choose the headlines for their stories. If your complaint is that a reasonable article has a sensational headline, take that up with their editor. Reporters also rarely have any power over the decision about whether a written correction gets issued. And in all cases, be resigned to the fact that you may not get a reply, but you've planted a seed, and it might help the next time a similar story comes around.

chance to refute the data in your own article or letter to the editor. (See the sidebar "The Media Are People, Too.") In today's age of "get the story out the quickest," we should become more skeptical of what we read in the paper or hear on the news. As the audience, we have the right to ask for well-researched, accurate stories, and so we shall. Try not to be hostile when writing to the author and the editor. Most of all, do not link to their story on your social media. If you do, you are giving them what they want: click traffic! Do not eat the bait.

Trolls

Recently, Deirdre was hired to speak at a dog boutique in Florida. The boutique was in a shopping center that was managed by a co-op board. A local person who openly disliked pit bulls called the shopping center and urged that the event be taken off its website. The board did so and then apologized to the boutique owner. This local person then went on to social media and began further disparaging pit bull advocates, blaming them for why children are harmed in dog bite incidents. Deirdre still gave her talk to a packed room and, naturally, this guy never showed up to learn.

This kind of knee-jerk social bullying is not uncommon these days. Don't allow bullying, but don't let the trolls shake your foundation, either. They are a rare and angry few.

Myths About Pit Bulls

There have probably been myths about pit bulls for as long as there have been pit bulls. Here's a story published in 1802 that circulated widely: One dog in a bull-baiting trial continued to hold on even as the owner amputated each of its feet to demonstrate its imperviousness to pain. Nowadays, the common myths tend to make bizarre claims about the pit bull's physical features that are so specific that the details may make them sound plausible. None of these have any basis in fact:

PIT BULLS HAVE "LOCKING JAWS."

If this were true, it would be easy to tell by examining the skull and jaw of a pit bull and comparing it to that of other dogs. The anatomy of dogs has been well studied and there's no evidence for any structure that would allow the jaws of a pit bull to lock.

PIT BULLS CAN HOLD ON WITH THEIR FRONT TEETH AND CHEW WITH THEIR BACK TEETH.

This is a rather venerable legend, according to Karen Delise, who traces it back to old myths that were circulated in the 1800s about bulldogs. Same as above, there's no anatomical difference in a pit bull jaw that would make this possible.

PIT BULLS HAVE EXTREME JAW STRENGTH AND BITE PRESSURE, FAR EXCEEDING THAT OF OTHER TYPES OF DOGS.

This statement is usually accompanied by some specific figure, such as 1,800 psi (pounds per square inch), which may sound scientific, but has no source in actual research. Published scientific research on bite force differences in dogs does exist, but does not differentiate by breed (for example, one recent paper looks at size and skull shape; breed is never mentioned). Such research reports such figures as, in one study, a mean of 256 Newtons (N)—the unit of measurement actually used in such studies—which converts to about 371 psi.

If those specific huge numbers aren't true, where did they come from? Bronwen Dickey speculates that they trace back to a 1969 medical journal article about dog bite wounds that gives a top figure of 450 psi for attack-trained German shepherds, with no information about how it was measured. Exaggerated versions of this figure began to appear in the media stories about dogs soon after.

Wherever they started, the numbers took on a life of their own and got bigger and bigger. It's interesting to note that the highest bite pressure recorded in a carnivore in the scientific literature was for the spotted hyena—4,500 N (1,011 psi). If a particular breed of dog truly bit with a pressure almost double that, that would be a scientific fact of great interest, and whoever had measured it would not be hiding it away where the source can't be easily found.

Unite and Conquer

Many dog advocacy groups exist. Some have social media followings of well over half a million people. When a troubling article comes up, or the need to rally support for a death row dog, where is everyone? Many groups work in isolation from each other. In an ideal world, if these groups combined intellect and numbers, there would be no more breed specific legislation.

pit bull people

We could never discuss all the ways to become an advocate for pit bulls and all the different ways you can get there, because there are probably as many paths as there are people. So, we'll end this book with the stories of just a few individuals who are making a difference, and hope they inspire you to find your own way.

Ken Foster: Just Get Started

Ken Foster has seen a lot of change, in his own life and in the pit bull community. He's now an official employee of Animal Care and Control of New York City, heading up its brand-new Community Dogs program. But when he started the Sula Foundation in 2008, he was a writer and a "total amateur dog rescuer," he remembers. "I just put up fliers and said, 'I'm starting a pit bull group; who wants to join me?'"

Foster was inspired to start his foundation after writing *The Dogs Who Found Me*, a memoir featuring his pit bull Sula. While promoting the book, he encountered many groups that rescued and advocated for pit bulls, and he was struck by the fact that there was no such organization in New Orleans when they were so many of the local dogs.

His initial concept for the group turned out to be ahead of its time. He didn't mean to start another rescue—the idea was to help existing organizations with promotion, fostering, and other support. "But everyone thought it was crazy—why would your organization help our organization?" he says. "So we started doing our own thing."

One lesson Foster learned is that patience is key to changing minds. "In New Orleans we had a woman who bred her dogs but would contact all their offspring's owners to let them know to come to our clinics to get vaccinated. And after about two years of coming for vaccines, she brought her dogs in to get spayed and neutered. I always tell people about her, because it is often about developing a long relationship and letting people come to their own decision on their own time."

And in the long term, he did get the organization to where he'd originally meant to be: "In the past couple years we ended up more where I wanted to start—instead of pulling shelter dogs and fostering, fostering dogs that are still part of the shelter system. That way we had our group of people promoting them and the shelter still promoting them and they got adopted much faster. But it took years to get to that point because the idea of collaborating in that way was so foreign to people at the time."

Another thing changed along the way, too: His group was no longer alone. "We started because no one was doing pit bull stuff," says Foster. "And now, everybody is doing pit bull stuff in New Orleans." Even breed-specific organizations for other breeds were willing to take in pit bulls, so with more support for rescuing individual dogs, he began to concentrate more on outreach and resource sharing.

As pit bull advocacy was changing in New Orleans, so was Ken. As his group shifted focus, he was considering moving back to New York for various reasons, and thinking about connections he'd made in the past. He'd done events for his book with what's now called Animal Care and Control (ACC), the nonprofit that runs the municipal shelter system in New York City. "They reached out to me because they were really trying to restructure themselves to be a better place for dogs, which means a better place for pit bulls since that's most of what comes into the shelter," Foster says. Their reputation was controversial at the time, and some warned him against participating, but that didn't put him off: "I said, 'But they're trying to change, and I admire that.'"

He thought that history might be useful, but expectations were low—as a writer, he was used to cobbling things together to stay afloat. Some friends had just bought a cheap house in a small town outside the city, and he figured if he sold his property in New Orleans he could do the same: "I could get a job at Starbucks, I thought, then approach the ACC, maybe do some contract work or something. Then I'd be helping the New York dogs, which are the first dogs I fell in love with."

So when he approached a staff member who happened to be at a conference in New Orleans, the response was a surprise: "How quickly can you get here?" Next thing he knew, he had a full-time job.

Like Foster's original idea for the Sula Foundation, the Community Dogs program isn't a rescue. Instead, its goal is to keep dogs from needing to be rescued by supporting their owners and helping them stay together. Especially in low-income neighborhoods, many people surrender their dogs reluctantly because of financial problems, issues with finding housing, and other problems that might be solvable with a little help. The program offers such services as low-cost vaccination and spaying/neutering, a pet food bank, and free training seminars.

The program isn't restricted to pit bulls, although that's a lot of what they see—at one recent event they vaccinated eighty-five dogs from pit bulls to Chihuahuas to a giant Newfie. It's a pleasant surprise to some that all dogs are treated the same. A young man passing by wondered what was going on.

"And you let pit bulls come?" the man asked nervously.

"Absolutely," Ken replied, and the man's face lit up with joy. He wasn't used to this kind of inclusion.

A writer is a better fit for a job like this than you might think, because creativity is so essential. ACC had never had this kind of program before, so Foster would be helping to build it from scratch. And even once something like this is up and running, new challenges are pretty much the only thing you can count on.

"You have to be creative," Foster says, "because one way or the other, trying to figure out how to stretch the money or how to reach a group of people we haven't been able to reach before, it's all about creativity."

Creativity is also necessary because being a longtime, experienced advocate doesn't mean you can keep doing things the same way you've always done them. Times change, and approaches need to change, too. For instance, the decision was made not to restrict the program to pit bulls specifically, even though those would be most of the dogs Foster would be working with. "We didn't want it to be a pit bull-specific job because that gives people the idea that there is something wrong with pit bulls," he says. That's an important issue for advocates to consider. After all, what we really want to see is a breed-neutral future, not one where pit bulls need special treatment, either positive or negative. "It's one of the challenges for those of us who've been in it for a long time: First of all, finding room for enthusiastic newcomers who maybe don't think the way we do, but also realizing that the line keeps shifting, which is a good thing, But it means we need to keep shifting what we do."

And now, as someone who started by posting a few fliers and having a meeting in a cafe, he's the sort of person those newcomers ask how to get started. No one's likely to duplicate his path exactly, but that's sort of the point of his advice to them: He didn't plan it that way himself.

"I tell them do what I did. I just got started," he says. "People want to wait for some moment of clarity, or for some understanding of exactly what they should be doing, or they feel like they need to have done this before. But you can start small and just build from one idea and give yourself permission to learn along the way."

Sophie Gamand: Look Into Their Eyes

Photographer Sophie Gamand didn't start her Flower Power project because she loved pit bulls. It was actually kind of the opposite.

When Gamand left France to follow her husband's job to New York in 2010, she left behind everything and everyone she knew. "When I arrived here, photography became a way to discover my new surroundings and connect with people," she says. "But quickly I realized I was photographing dogs more than people. I think I was super shy, and there was the language barrier. Photographing dogs was easier."

She also began to learn about dog rescue and sheltering: "In Europe we don't really have that many shelters—it's not such a huge issue over there. I had never heard of such numbers as here. I became familiar with that. and I decided right away I wanted to be helping."

But as she volunteered taking photos at a shelter, she found herself reacting very differently to certain dogs. "Each time

they'd bring a pit bull for a shoot, I'd be, like, 'Uh, okay, let's sit over there. okay, done, bye!'" she recalls. "I'd never want to engage with them too much and I was super tense."

She traces the reaction to the time she was attacked by a dog as a child. "It was a dog that belonged to some of my friends who drove me to school, so every morning I would ring the bell and the dog would basically go crazy behind the gate. It was a dog that definitely had issues and his owners should have known better. And one day they opened the gate too early and the dog lunged at me and mauled me."

That dog wasn't a pit bull—they are banned in France—it was a Briard, a large herding breed. But the experience made her uncomfortable with similar large, energetic dogs, even though she loved animals and at one point wanted to grow up to be a vet.

You think it wouldn't help that some of her experiences with pit bulls since moving to the United States were quite negative, but surprisingly that was what started her thinking in a different direction. Gamand volunteered rescuing dogs in Puerto Rico, in a rural area plagued with crime, drugs, dogfighting, and a lot of stray pit bull-type dogs. Once, two of them attacked her and the dogs she was caring for. "I physically had to pull them off the dogs they were attacking, which is the stupidest thing to do, but I was on autopilot," she says. "I remember thinking, okay, I'm just going to lose my hands now."

She didn't lose her hands, but something changed in her heart.

In fact, she knew these two local dogs and sometimes fed them because their owner would go away and leave them for weeks without food. As she chased them away, she realized how miserable they looked. "They were malnourished, they had horrible mange. One was limping from an old car injury that was never treated," Gamand says. "This poor dog was limping back to his 'home' and he turned around and looked at me, looking so guilty . . . I will never forget that image of seeing them and feeling so sorry for them, and feeling like it was so unfair that people would put dogs in situations like this, setting them up for horrible accidents to happen. I think that triggered something in me about pit bulls."

That "something" came to fruition about a year and a half later, when she found herself back at the shelter, uneasy about photographing another pit bull. "One day, I realized: This is so stupid. These dogs haven't done anything to me. I've gone through a dog attack from another breed, I've gone through breaking up a fight between dogs. I can handle this."

She'd been thinking she wanted to do a project with a particular subset of shelter dogs, so she decided pit bulls would be it. This would be both a personal challenge and something where she could help dogs that were in particular need.

Artistically, she knew the photos would have to be portraits. "In my work, I focus on headshots," she says. "I feel a very strong connection to the face of dogs—not the body language so much, not the dog as an animal, but the dog as an individual." Her par-

ticular idea for the portraits, though, was definitely the personal challenge she was looking for: Putting flower crowns on the dogs meant getting unnervingly up close and personal. "The first crown I put on the first pit bull, I was basically a few inches away from their face. I'm sitting facing the dog and tying something to the head, probably one of the most threatening things you can do to a dog you don't know."

She stepped away quickly and grabbed her camera, figuring the best-case scenario was that the dog would be eating the flowers.

But that wasn't at all what she saw. "She was just sitting there looking at me—there was something so dignified about her. Her eyes were so soulful and there was so much sadness at the same time."

The series went viral immediately and has become so successful that, after starting as a side project, it's become pretty much her full-time brand. But why did it work so well? Gamand, who based her idea on baroque portraiture, explains that the photos have more complexity than you'd expect from the idea of dogs with flowers on their heads. "In art, what succeeds is oppositions," she says. "You take a scary dog and you put cute flowers on them and they look sad—then you have three different dimensions that you wouldn't expect to be together, because a dog wearing flowers should be the silliest thing you've ever seen. But if the dog looks sad, it has the extra dimension that I feel really conveys the message."

She also takes the photographs in a way that evokes certain particular emotions. "I wanted a sense of nostalgia. That's why they're a little blurry, a little foggy. I wanted them to look like vintage images faded by the sun and elements. For me it was about thinking about what is being lost and the lives that are being destroyed."

And the fact that the photos are portraits—that you look right into the dog's eyes—is vital to their impact as well. "I wanted them to evoke a lot of emotions and to create a sense of vulnerability and remind people that these are fragile lives. You have to connect with the life behind that face. The series is meant to challenge people to look at pit bulls from a different perspective—to challenge you to look at those eyes and tell me you're not feeling sorry for them. Tell me you feel the way we treat them is fair and okay."

Steffen Baldwin: A Sense of Purpose

Lots of people say they didn't rescue their pit bull—their pit bull rescued them. Steffen Baldwin's personal story is a lot like that, but on a much bigger scale.

When Baldwin interviewed for a job as director of a rural Ohio shelter in 2008, he didn't have a background working with animals, but that was okay with them. The shelter was doing pretty well with the animals—its problem was that it was failing financially. "I landed this job strictly from my nonprofit and fund-raising experience," he says. "Their biggest focus was to find someone good at fund-raising." Baldwin thought he knew exactly what he was getting into. "I had done my research on this organization and they had over a 90 percent placement rate. They said, when they did their fund-raising, 'We never euthanize an animal for time or space, only medical or behavioral reasons.' That's what they said over and over again." So, he was taken aback when he was being given a tour and came across some pit bulls being kept behind closed doors. "I saw these really adorable, blocky-headed wiggly butts, their gigantic face was one big smile," he says. "I asked about those dogs and the operations manager said, "We can't adopt them out, they're going to have to be put down.'"

What he hadn't known was that at the time in Ohio, there was a statewide law classifying pit bulls as vicious. So, while the shelter did place 90 percent of adoptable animals, the secret behind that statistic was that pit bulls were automatically classified as unadoptable.

the pit bull life

Baldwin hadn't encountered this kind of breed-specific prejudice before. "I grew up outside of LA, on welfare in the projects, in a very diverse neighborhood, and there were a lot of big dogs around. Breed discrimination was not really something I was familiar with. I was afraid of scary dogs, but they came in all shapes and sizes as far as I remember growing up." There wasn't much he could do at first, but in 2012 the state law was eliminated. While individual jurisdictions could still have their own breed-specific ordinance, his locality didn't have one, so he went to the shelter board and tried to get the pit bull policy changed. Three times over the course of five years, the result was the same. "Each time they let me put together a committee," he says, "it always recommended to adopt them out, and they always shot it down."

Baldwin was also having problems in his personal life, going through a deep depression after getting divorced. "I was searching for something that was important, that I could latch onto for my own sense of purpose," he says. One thing he did to help himself pull through was take on the local humane law enforcement agent position, which had been vacant for a year. "I started going out on these calls every night after my job was over, rather than going to the bar as I had the first few months after my marriage ended."

The experience was eye-opening. "Surprisingly, even though we were in a rural area, when they were dogs, most of them involved pit bull-type dogs," he says. Despite being director of the shelter, he'd had no opportunity to see how many pit bulls were around, for a couple of reasons. One was that the shelter didn't take pit bulls as owner surrenders, only as strays. The other was that they hadn't come in on humane law cases, either. "My old agents never seized animals, never brought charges. The report was always, everything was fine. They always worked something out. It wasn't till I started enforcing these laws that they started coming into the shelter."

More enforcement ought to have been good news for dogs, but of course it created a big problem for the pit bulls. "I was doing what I thought was important by enforcing these laws—but I was taking them to the shelter where I couldn't adopt them out," Baldwin says. "It was a real quandary—why are you rescuing the animal, if it's only going to be put down somewhere else?" The shelter board let him place pit bulls with rescues, but local rescues were often full or didn't have the resources to deal with a particular dog's issues. He once had to drive an abandoned pit bull 1,600 miles to Best Friends Animal Society in Utah to find a place for it.

Along with the conflict over pit bulls, eventually his more active humane law enforcement became an issue as well. While this might seem strange to animal-loving urbanites, the shelter was concerned that it might have a bad effect on donations. "Anywhere rural with an agricultural base, there's a battle between ag and the humane community," he says. "There's always this fear that anything that animal welfare is going to do, that it's a slippery slope to dismantling the dairy business." Baldwin finally

decided that to do the job the way he thought it needed to be done
he'd have to go out on his own, and he formed his own nonprofit,
Animal Cruelty Task Force of Ohio (ACT Ohio).

ACT Ohio's officers have full police powers to enforce animal
cruelty laws, but much of what they deal with is ignorance and
lack of resources. Education is a high priority because sometimes ignorance can do as much damage as abuse. He tells of

one woman who treated her little pit bull for worms with her interpretation of an old farmer's remedy. "They were feeding chewing tobacco raw to this puppy, not realizing that it costs more than the dewormer would have cost at a vet," he says. "They were thinking they were saving money because they didn't have the money to go to the vet and they almost killed the dog out of pure ignorance."

Frequently rather than seizing animals, ACT Ohio is problem-solving to keeping people together with their beloved pets. Baldwin says that often the person's problem is "too much month at the end of their money. I've been on calls where the person is as skinny as the dog." It's important not to jump to conclusions, even when a situation looks bad at first glance. In one case he got a call because a pit bull was reportedly living in a car in the summertime. He found not just a dog in a car with food and water and the windows rolled down, but an owner who was between a rock and a hard place. "Long story short, nineteen-year-old kid, fiancée, one baby and a baby on the way, lost his job and apartment. He went to his dad's trailer, but his dog and his dad's dog didn't get along."

It was clear to Baldwin that this wasn't abuse. "You can't leave your dog in a car, but was he trying to hurt this dog? No. He was trying to figure the situation out," he says. "It clear there was a strong bond. So, at that point the goal was assistance—how do we keep these two together?"

Unfortunately, a couple of other attempts at living situations failed, so finally the owner called and said he had to surrender the dog. But the story has a happy ending. "I told him, 'She is going up for adoption, but if you get back on your feet, call me and you can have her back.' And, sure enough, that's what happened two months later." The dog was still in foster care at the time, so Baldwin checked out the owner's new place and his employment situation, and they were reunited.

Baldwin says that humane agents really do more of that kind of work than the high-profile cruelty cases, but you just don't hear as much about it. For one thing, they want to respect people's privacy—no one wants to be plastered all over the internet because they don't have enough money to feed their dog. For another, they have no choice but to publicize the cruelty cases, because they need to ask for support to care for them, and it can take thousands of dollars to care for an animal seized in such a case.

So, it's a good thing his background is in fund-raising—particularly in his county, where there's essentially no financial support for his work. By law—a very old law—agents are only paid $25 per month. There are no zeros accidentally left out there—it's really only $25.

"It's an interesting dichotomy," he says. "We have full police powers, but we go through only twenty hours of training. You're not given a badge; you have to buy that on your own. You're given the power, but then it's just go off and enforce these laws—there's no oversight and no support." In fact, although he started his nonprofit with a nice donation, he's had to cobble together ways to support himself. He was interim director at a small shelter, and did side jobs like installing insulation for his landlady. Only now, going into the third year, has he been able to start drawing a very modest salary.

Frustrated that people seem more interested in passing laws than funding their enforcement, it was perhaps inevitable that he's been drawn into working on legislative issues. Tough laws attract support, he says, "but if you are in a state where over half of the landmass has literally no one with the enforcement ability and authority, you can have all the penalties in the world and if no one is out investigating, they won't do any good." And it's the same problem if there are officers, but they're paid so little that they can only work in their spare time. "When things go crazy on social media about a dog or an animal being abused, people ask, 'Where's the humane agent?' Well, in rural Ohio, the humane agent is probably at his day job. You have an emergency? Well, sorry, they just clocked into their shift at Honda."

Along with working with legislators to try to solve that problem, he has been drawn into the problem of breed-specific legislation. While Baldwin founded ACT Ohio to do humane law enforcement, people perceived the organization a little differently. "We weren't a pit bull rescue, but it turned out that about eighty percent of our cases fell into that category," he says. "So, we got a following that saw us as pit bull rescuers."

Baldwin found himself providing testimony on both local ordinances and state animal welfare bills. He helped in one town where a breed-specific law was replaced with a breed-neutral dangerous dog ordinance, but he was often frustrated at the state level. "I watched many of those bills fail, all for political reasons. It came down to who had the best lobbyists and the most influence." And the sad thing he discovered is that the people with the most influence when it came to these bills weren't experts about animals, but political action committees (PACs). The good news, though? "It is ridiculously easy to form a PAC," he says. "You need three people at least, but pretty much anyone can do it in a matter of minutes." He realized that form-

ing a committee would allow him to raise funds for lawsuits and other needs, and would allow him to work on banning breed-specific legislation at the state level, instead of fighting it one locality at a time. And it would elevate his status in the eyes of lawmakers. "When working with politicians, it gives the impression of a different degree of legitimacy, being a political action committee."

The general public probably doesn't see it that way, but sometimes different strategies are needed for different audiences. In other ways, though, he says that his success on social media and with lawmakers is based on the same principles. "Politicians don't listen to ranting and ravings. They don't listen to emotions. I try to keep it positive and be nonjudgmental and nonaccusatory and matter-of-fact," he says. "When you get so wrapped up in your emotion, I think you can lose the message and lessen your efficacy."

Brad Croft: Put That Drive to Work

To Brad Croft, training shelter dogs for police work was a totally logical idea, but there was some emotion behind it, too. He knows how it feels to be treated the way people had treated them.

"Everything I did was full blast," he says of himself as a boy. "No means yes and I'm hell on wheels. My adoptive parents couldn't control me—they started sending me away, letting other people deal with me." He sees something of himself in the high-energy, high-drive dogs that can be too much for pet owners but that are perfect for this work. "These dogs, like myself, we get shipped off to be somebody else's problem. I want to find those dogs and I want to help them succeed, because they can. When you focus that energy, it's phenomenal what you get out of it."

UniversalK9 in San Antonio, Texas, started in 2010 doing the same thing as all the other companies: importing specially bred purebred dogs from Europe, training them, and selling them to police departments and the military. That's just how the business works, but something about it didn't make sense to him. "I know that it does not take any specific breed of dog to do this work," he says. "All it takes is a damn good dog; it doesn't matter if it's a mutt or a pit bull or a German shepherd. I also knew there are shelters all around the United States bulging at the seams with capable dogs. So what the hell am I doing?"

He also knew that there were plenty of smaller police departments that couldn't afford the something like $20,000 per dog plus the cost to train the officer. It just made sense to put these two facts together. "I can start rescuing these dogs and helping these underfunded police departments and it'll be a fantastic thing," he thought. The deal he offered with the shelter dogs was that the dog and its training were free—the police departments just had to pay for the officer to come for handler training, so the company could break even. The idea took off to the extent that last year his originally for-profit company turned nonprofit.

But even as the program was getting in the news all over the country, something still wasn't right. At Austin Pets Alive, he found himself testing a lot of pit bulls, since that was so much of what came into the shelter. "Man, these dogs are good; I wish I could use them, because they're fantastic," he said to his contact there. "But I can't get a police department to take them because of the stigma. What can we do?'

A problem like that doesn't last long in the face of Croft's high-drive, high-energy mind. He had the idea for an offer that was too good to refuse: If a police department would take a pit bull, not only the dog and its training would be free, but the handler's training would be free also.

Turns out it's amazing what the word *free* can do to get people to stop for a minute and rethink their prejudices. When he does a demo for a new class of officers with one of his shelter pit bulls, they can't help doing the math: "They see me working a pit bull and this light switch goes off in their brain: 'They're doing the same things as these dogs we're paying for. What the hell are we doing?'"

With the financial support of the Animal Farm Foundation, pit bulls are now getting placed in police departments and showing what they can do. They're trained to sniff out narcotics or explosives and to track people, so they can find a lost child or elderly person. They're friendly with the public and great ambassadors for the breed. There's one job they don't do, though. "We do not use pit bulls for bite work," he says.

Why? Despite all the myths about the pit bull's bite and ferocity, Croft says they're just not good at it. "They're not going to be able to hold the person down, they're not big enough, their bite is not as good as a German shepherd or Belgian Malinois. And most of them don't want to bite. If they were good at it, I would put them to work at it, but they're not." At the other jobs, though, he says they're awesome. One recent graduate, Kiah, who was placed in the police department in Poughkeepsie, New York, Croft calls "one of the top three dogs I've ever worked with. Very trainable, very motivated; she's got a great nose." And, he says, "There's not a mean bone in that dog's body."

It just makes sense: dogs are saved, police departments get great dogs, and it helps the reputation of pit bulls and shelter dogs in general. But Croft has a bigger goal in mind as well. "If we place a dog in every single state that has BSL, guess what happens with BSL?" he says. Police are the ones that enforce the laws, and if they don't think breed-specific laws make sense, imagine the weight that will carry. "If you can convince the police, the police will convince the city council. If the police say, 'You are wrong about these dogs,' slowly but surely, it's going to knock that right out."

Candice Miller: Foster a Future

Candice Miller wasn't always an advocate for pit bulls. When she was a young girl, her beloved family dog, a husky, lost its life to two roaming dogs believed to be pit bulls. The trauma from this incident left her emotionally scarred and sure that she would never want to adopt a pit bull of her own. Candice grew up with three Labs that were her best friends, along with chickens and goats. As a teenager, she adopted a shelter mix named Allie. Allie was a six-week-old puppy and Candice herself was a young mother, with a son who was two at the time. She then adopted Lucky, a nine-month-old chocolate Lab, from college kids that had left Lucky crated around the clock. Next came Bella, a purebred Pomeranian that Candice couldn't say no to after an employee of hers explained that the dog lived in the bathroom 24/7, was fed Taco Bell, and who was maddeningly kicked by the young girl's dad, leaving her with a broken leg. The young girl begged Candice to take the dog or she herself would be kicked out of her home.

Candice suddenly had three dogs and two young children. Her son was sixteen years old when he offered to help a homeless skateboarder friend by taking his six-week-old puppy home. The puppy was full of worms and thankfully was pulled from the situation before he was fed cigarette butts to attempt to deworm him. Candice's son, Miles, brought the young puppy home and hid him in his bedroom. She'd soon learn that the puppy was not only adorable but was also quite sick. She agreed to help get the puppy healthy as long as Miles kept the puppy hidden from her husband. Candice recalled having been mauled by a Saint Bernard when she was four years old and was curious why she was not concerned around those dogs, but still found herself nervous around this little puppy once she realized it was a pit bull mix. She knew it was an irrational fear, so she took to the Internet to research these dogs fur-

ther. Unfortunately, her search engine turned up many negative "facts" and stories from anti-dog rhetoric sites. She had to work hard to find good information about pit bulls. Miles and Candice successfully hid the puppy for three weeks as the puppy recovered until one day her husband asked whether there was a cat in their yard, because there were "weird poops" in the grass. When Candice came clean, he couldn't help but exclaim, "He's a pit bull? But he's so cute!" He had grown up with Brittany spaniels and had less experience than Candice with multidog households.

Over the next week or so, Candice and her family decided that they'd like to hold onto this puppy after they realized that he was "twenty times more solid of a dog (in personality) than Lucky the purebred Lab. It was so eye-opening!" The skateboarder friend agreed to let them keep the puppy, and he'd now be known as Roofus.

Candice was working long hours in retail management and found herself getting stuck in a dark mental space. Her work life had become so toxic that she wasn't sure if she wanted to continue living. The only place that she found solace was in the company of her family and her dogs. She begged her husband to help her take a mental health break from her day job.

She describes spending her entire life with dogs as a feeling of being on the level with them, "like I'm with my peeps!" She saw that the Sacramento SPCA was offering volunteer classes and knew that this felt like the right opportunity for some soul searching and spiritual cleansing. As she began volunteering, she noticed very quickly that most of the volunteers were older and were not as comfortable handling the larger dogs, such as the pit bulls. She knew that they were being overlooked and wanted to work more with these dogs to give them a chance, even though she was still quite nervous about them as a whole. One afternoon, she talked herself into walking a very large pit bull. When she took him out of the kennel, he surprised her by lying down and being very affectionate with her. Even though he had no manners, she knew this was a good dog. She immersed herself in the healing power of dogs and volunteering. She was in awe of the resilience in the character of these dogs who had often been through so many dark days of their own but still appeared so happy, playful, and appreciative. She believes that "it's good for every person to spend just a couple of hours at their local shelter. So, that they can take that and go, 'Oh my gosh, I was just at the shelter and they have puppies!' People don't know that there are puppies at the shelter. You can even put yourself on a list for puppies. It's not just the pound anymore."

She knew that she was there volunteering for them, but started to realize that it was healing for her because it allowed her to be present like the dogs, to live in the moment as dogs do. This is when she realized that she was falling in love with pit bull-type dogs. She began watching the "facts" that she had read about on the anti-pit bull pages become mythological. "I think that the best thing to understand is that I didn't start out as a pit bull advocate. I didn't like pit bulls. I had the same sense of them as the general population. I literally said I would never own a pit bull in my life. It's the power of education that changed me." She knew she had been misinformed and wanted to spread the positive shift that she had experienced with the world.

During this emotional shift, a very sweet dog arrived at the shelter. He wouldn't stop shaking and walked flat on his belly. It would take a while just to get him from the kennel to the outside yard. When she finally coerced him to get out into the yard, he pushed his way onto her lap and sat on her while she sat on a bench. He spent the next few months at the shelter and was becoming a well-adjusted dog, but was oddly still not adopted by anyone. Then the shelter had a special Free Cat Adoption day that would decide this poor dog's fate forever. A child was roaming through the kennels and kicked at his cage. He lunged forward and barked at the child. Unfortunately, Candice wasn't at the shelter when the shelter staff had to pull him from the adoptable floor and bring him back to the holding area for euthanasia. He was given seven days with the only option to leave the shelter through a volunteer, a rescue pull, or by being put to death. The shelter had a very strict policy about any level of "aggressive behavior," and even though he found himself startled by a young boy, it was to his detriment to have reacted the way that he did.

When Candice came into the shelter for her volunteer shift, she noticed that his cage was empty. Elated, she ran to the front to find out if her favorite boy had finally been adopted. She was quickly defeated when she found out what happened and that he was on borrowed time. She contacted every rescue in the region and wasn't able to get him pulled. She knew this dog would only live if she could convince the shelter and her family to let him come home. The shelter told her that she needed to bring in the entire pack to make sure it was a good match. She wasn't sure what Lucky the Lab would do when introduced, but when they brought out Kilo, he ran forward crying and yelping at the first sight of his beloved Candice. He didn't pay any attention to the other dogs. She described the moment as "magical." Her daughter, Julia, was thirteen at the time and she was just as in love with him as Roofus was. A photo was sent to Candice's husband and he knew that they were about to have four dogs again (as Allie had passed shortly beforehand).

This prompted her to start a social media page on Instagram to share her rescue stories and experiences. "Because Kilo was a dad, he gravitates to the puppies. He raised Penny after I pulled her out of a bad situation at three days old. Kilo taught her how to be a dog. That's when our account exploded because people were watching this rescued death-row pit bull raise this abandoned three-day-old pit bull. He was being so sweet with her, and so mothering, it was really incredible to witness for myself let alone being able to share this awesome nature of a pit bull was cool. That's where our account really exploded and I'm glad it was for a good reason."

Their page now has over 300,000 dedicated followers that enjoy watching the relationship with their family, both dogs and humans. Candice noted of her following that "people liked the friendship that the dogs made." It turned out that Kilo, who was named Kiko at the shelter, had belonged to a drug dealer in town. A fan recognized him and knew his backstory. Kilo was afraid of everything and Candice found herself outfitting him in a ThunderShirt™ simply to cope with a howling windstorm.

Her story of rescuing dogs and especially pit bull-type dogs has prompted fans of her page to shadow her work and begin their own efforts in their local shelters by volunteering, fund-raising, fostering, promoting spay and neuter clinics, and adopting.

It is Candice's hope that her page will continue to inspire people. She and her family recently moved to Oregon and have purchased farmland to increase their rescue and fostering efforts. "I would have never left California because that's where my family is . . . but we're kind of in doggy paradise in Eugene, Oregon." Miller is a California girl who has transplanted herself into a new state because of her motivation to do more for the dogs. Her efforts were limited in California since real estate costs are egregious. The property that they've been able to secure in Oregon backs up to thousands of acres of protected forest. Leaving her extended family behind in California was a bittersweet choice, but her heart is happiest when she is doing more for animals in need. It's a tough sacrifice, but she is excited that she is able to develop their property into a haven for unwanted animals.

Their new home is being outfitted with a special room just for foster dogs and will eventually have a barn for additional dogs as needed. She is filing for her 501(c)3 and hopes that her passion for rescue will continue to spread positively across their fan pages. "I'm excited at the thought of expanding. I'll be able to foster anything that comes my way. We're going to be getting our rescue license in the coming months. Out on the property we have this pasture and we're hoping to be able to build actual individual literal houses for dogs with their own backyards in that part."

Roofus and Kilo now help socialize new foster dogs in their home. "When you foster, everything is paid for by the shelter or rescue, it's all covered. From the get-go, we provided our own food, potty pads, kennels, and everything has been funded by our own means. I did the Amazon Wish List so people can see where their money is going. Other than vetting, we cover everything ourselves. It's to the dogs one hundred percent and that's how I want it. My poor husband works a lot and hard so that we can keep saving dogs and he's completely okay with it at this point. It's pretty beautiful."

Candice wants to inspire people who might be losing their will to live. She wants them to take a breath, go to their local shelter, and walk a dog. This simple and small contribution has lasting positive effects, and, in her eyes, has saved her life in addition to the lives of many animals. Candice, like so many others, has found herself as an "accidental advocate." She hopes that her "misfit family of reject dogs" can help even the most hard-line pit bull hater understand her past experience. "From the get-go, I got all the reject dogs that are unwanted or too sick, like the ones that we have—Lucky, Bella, all of them." She doesn't believe in sugarcoating and often warns her followers to not take on more than they can. "Don't go out and try to do what I am doing. If you're not able to rehab them and take care of them then you're just creating more problems."

Even she once had disdain for these misunderstood dogs. Now she is able to effect change on a personal level and through the power of social media. Her beloved children and husband help support her daily efforts and look forward to their eventual growth into a full-scale rescue. In the meantime, she proudly shared that, "It's a dream come true for me to have a dedicated foster room because I can help more dogs, more puppies."

Stacey Coleman: Stand Together

Stacey Coleman was living in Indianapolis, working for a publishing company, and going to school to be a certified sign language interpreter. Then one day in 2001, a pit bull hitched a ride that took her to an entirely unexpected destination.

She was driving down the street on her way to lunch when she saw a dog running down the sidewalk. "Someone was getting ready to kick the dog because it was trying to grab their bag of fast food," she says. "I threw open the door and said, 'Hey, little dog, what are you doing?' The dog looked at me, ran over as fast as she could, jumped in, hit the passenger seat, bounced into the backseat, and sat there smiling."

Sounds like an easy, successful outcome to a compassionate impulse—Coleman didn't even have to work to catch the dog. But now she took a closer look, and her thoughts went wild: "I think that's a pit bull. I think I'm supposed to be afraid of that dog. Holy crap, there's a pit bull in the backseat. I'd better get out, I'm going to die."

While the dog continued sitting there wagging her tail, Coleman stopped the car, got out, and called a humane society. They came to get the dog and that would probably have been the end of it if she hadn't had another helpful notion. "But then I think, they're a nonprofit. I should give them money to pay for her care. I called them said, 'I'll write the check for whatever she needs.'" The answer was a shock: Never mind, because the dog was going to be euthanized. That was their policy on pit bulls.

Despite her initial reaction to the dog, she decided to fight back. "I have no idea why I did this, but I couldn't accept what they were going to do with this dog," she says. "Once I got my head in order, she seemed like a lovely dog." Coleman's spurof-the-moment inspiration was to try changing her story—she told them she'd lied, it was really her dog and she wanted it back. They didn't buy it, but she found out that there was a seven-day stray hold period.

She got an attorney, and days later they went to pick up the dog, which was preceded by a meeting with the director, the chair of the board, and their lawyer. "They required I sign a paper stating that I would not sue the agency when this dog severely injured or killed someone—or me."

Coleman signed, went home, and waited to see what the dog she named Gertie did that was so scary. She quickly discovered that rather than be a fighter, this dog was a peacemaker. "She wouldn't let the cats fight She'd go all Oprah on them—she'd separate them and not let them fight."

Gertie was just as good with other species. One time, Coleman heard a small animal screaming and went running to see what was wrong. "She's lying there with a mouse between her paws and the cats are lined up around her and she's protecting it from the cats." Once when she was volunteering at a refugee center after 9/11, she took temporary custody of five children from Afghan-istan. When she brought them home, everyone, including her-self, was traumatized. "I'm crying, the kids are crying, they all have PTSD, none of them speak English. I don't have kids—what the hell am I going to do with five kids?"

She recalls standing there helpless as the youngest, a five-year-old, sat on the floor crying, till Gertie came to the rescue. "Gertie walks over to him, turns around, backs up her bottom, and sits in his lap," she says. "He puts his little arms around her, puts his head against her back, and stops crying. That's just the kind of dog she was."

Being that kind of dog is no protection from breed prejudice, though, and Coleman found herself having to fight for her dog again after a terrible incident when a little girl in a stroller was left outside a drug dealer's house and a dog came out and mauled her. "From that, the mayor of Indianapolis decides he's going to round up and kill all the pit bulls in the city. I'm thinking about how this mayor was going to take my dog away and I decided I was going to fight this."

She'd never been involved in city politics before and knew nothing about BSL at the time. She started by getting to know all of the city council members. "I marched into their offices, I called, I sent e-mails, I collected as much information as I could so I understood the lay of the land—what people were thinking and what information I needed to bring. I quickly realized that I needed to be the smartest person in the room on this subject, so I needed to get my information correct."

Coleman reached out to experts across the country and also did her own research on the local level. "My common sense told me that if there really is a problem with dogs running loose or with dogs injuring people, it doesn't occur in a vacuum; there are other things going wrong, too." She organized meetings for the public, media, and city councilors, and at one she did a presentation where she mapped out the dog complaints that came into animal control. "I charted that on a map of the city and then overlaid some other societal issues—where there were the most burglary claims, the most assaults reported," she says. "And what do you know, they matched up. And what do you know, it was very much concentrated in zip codes avoided by the police and social services."

There wasn't really a dog problem, Coleman argued. "It was a larger symptom of a failure of the city," she says. "When you start having the conversation, it turns out that animal control is not enforcing the laws that protect us from negligent dog owners, and they're also not enforcing the laws that protect the kids on the street from the drug dealers; they're also not protecting the homeowners that are constantly plagued by vandalism. I'm not conceding that dogs are dangerous, but if you think they are, look at where your calls are coming from and look at the other things going wrong in these communities. So, shame on you, city leaders, for not addressing the problems and the challenges that these communities are facing."

Identifying the problem is only ever the first step, though. She knew people needed to work together, and that started with the ones who were on her side. She said to her volunteers, "We can argue with each other and call each other names in this room and go toe to toe, but, by god, when we step out in public, we had better be unified in our message." Her message to politicians was basically the same; honest, contentious discussion was fine, "as long as we can agree on what is best going forward for the city," she says. "When you have that kind of honest conversation with people, you have better trust going forward."

Coleman also reached out to people involved in incidents with dogs. With the owners, "I would go to their house and knock on their door and say, 'Your dog injured someone, and this is what the fallout is going to be for me as another dog owner in the city because this is the climate. I want to know what happened so when the media comes to me, I know the story. If you're responsible please take responsibility, because I don't want to take responsibility for your neglect.'" She did the same on the other side, and this gained her some surprising allies. One was a woman whose son was seriously bitten when a neighbor's dog dug out under a fence. "I talked to her and said, 'It must have been terrifying, I'm sure it was awful. But when you say, *A pit bull did it*, I get the blame, and my dog gets the blame. Do you really think we are dangerous?' The woman said no, she didn't, so Coleman said to her, 'Can we stand up together and say, *City leaders, it's your responsibility to find a solution that supports all of us, instead of creating a fall guy that makes it easier to do your job?*'" The woman agreed, and they spoke together at the next city council meeting.

An important lesson from her experience is that bringing people together makes it impossible for a politician to divide and conquer. "Don't let anybody imply that there's an 'us' versus 'them,' because everyone wants to live in a safe community," she says. "I want to live in a safe community, the person whose kid was injured by a dog wants to live in a safe community. That's what we have in common."

In the end, the legislation didn't make it out of committee, and when it was proposed again the following year, "no one even really looked at it twice," she says. Then the mayor lost the next election, so Coleman could have been free to relax and call an end to her involvement in pit bull advocacy. But she'd caught the attention of Jane Berkey of Animal Farm Foundation, "because I was always in the newspaper shaking my fist in righteous indignation. She contacted me and asked if I had any interest, and I said I'd be there in two weeks." Now executive director, she's been there since 2008.

Coleman is amazed at the progress she's seen since Gertie came into her life. She recalls a time years ago when she was talking to someone from a Lab rescue about the prejudice pit bull owners faced. "She said we have the opposite problem—people see our dogs and set their children loose and say, 'Go get the doggy,' and the dogs are freaked out by it," she recalls. Now instead of people crossing the street when they see her dogs, her experience is often much more like that. Recently she was sitting on a bench with her foster dog, feeding him treats, watching people go by, to get him used to busy places.

"Somebody stopped to pet the dog, then somebody else stopped to pet the dog . . . pretty soon he was absolutely flooded with people standing around wanting to touch him." While that's the sort of thing that can sometimes be a problem, it's a remarkable problem to have. She says, "I can't even believe how far we've come."

bibliography

Introduction: Picture a Pit Bull

Keller, Helen. *The Story of My Life*. New York: Doubleday, Page & Company, 1905.

PBS website for Ken Burns's film *Horatio's Wheel*. "The Sidekick." www.pbs
.org/horatio/wheel/#bud. Accessed April 19 2016.

"Pete the bulldog Gets a Victim." *New York Times*, May 10, 1907.

"Pete Now Is Banished: President's bulldog Exiled After Chasing Senator up
a Tree." *Washington Post*, June 12, 1907.

"Stubby of A.E.F. Enters Valhalla." *New York Times*, April 4, 1926.

Chapter 1. What Is a Pit Bull?

Coppinger, Raymond, and Lorna Coppinger. *Dogs: A New Understanding of
Canine Origin, Behavior and Evolution*. Chicago: University of Chicago
Press, 2001.

Hearne, Vicki. *Bandit: Dossier of a Dangerous Dog*. New York: Harper Collins, 1991.

Jessup, Diane. *The Working Pit Bull*. Neptune City, New Jersey: T. F. H. Publications, 1995.

Olson, K. R., J. K. Levy, B. Norby, M. M. Crandall, J. E. Broadhurst, S. Jacks, R. C. Barton, and M. S. Zimmerman. "Inconsistent Identification of Pit Bull–Type Dogs by Shelter Staff." *Veterinary Journal* (2015) 206 (2015): 197–202.

Staffordshire bull terrier Club Of America website. "Nature of the Beast." www.sbtca.com/index.php?option=com_content&view=article&id=3&Itemid=3. Accessed April 16, 2016.

Voith, Victoria L., Elizabeth Ingram, Katherine Mitsouras, and Kristopher Irizarry. "Comparison of Adoption Agency Breed Identification and DNA Breed Identification of Dogs." *Journal of Applied Animal Welfare Science* 12, no. 3 (2009): 253–62.

Voith, Victoria L., Rosalie Trevejo, Seana Dowling-Guyer, Colette Chadik, Amy Marder, Vanessa Johnson, and Kristopher Irizarry. "Comparison of Visual and DNA Breed Identification of Dogs and Inter-Observer Reliability." *American Journal of Sociological Research* 3, no. 2, (2013): 17–29. doi: 10.5923/j.sociology.20130302.02.

Chapter 2. How We Saw Pit Bulls Then

Delise, Karen. *The Pit Bull Placebo: The Media, Myths, and Politics of Canine Aggression*. Anubis Publishing, 2007.

Duffy, Deborah L., Yuying Hsu, and James A. Serpell, "Breed Differences in Canine Aggression." *Applied Animal Behaviour Science* 114 (2008): 441–60.

MacNeil-Allcock, A., N. M. Clarke, R. A. Ledger, and D. Fraser. "Aggression, Behaviour, and Animal Care Among Pit Bulls and Other Dogs Adopted from an Animal Shelter." *Animal Welfare* 20 (2011): 463–68.

Orlean, Susan. *Rin Tin Tin: The Life and the Legend.* New York: Simon & Schuster, 2011.

Ott, Stefanie A., DVM, Esther Schalke, DVM, Amelie M. von Gaertner, DVM, and Hansjoachim Hackbarth, DVM, PhD. "Is There a Difference? Comparison of golden retrievers and Dogs Affected by Breed-Specific Legislation Regarding Aggressive Behavior." *Journal of Veterinary Behavior: Clinical Applications and Research* 3 (2008): 134–40.

Reisner, Ilana R., DVM, PhD, DACVB, Katherine A. Houpt, VMD, PhD, DACVB, and Frances S. Shofer, PhD. "National Survey of Owner-Directed Aggression in English springer spaniels." *Journal of the American Veterinary Medical Association* 227, no. 10 (November 15, 2005: 1594–603.

"Straight from the G.A.S. Tank" column, *The Progress*, Clearfield, PA, Tuesday evening, February 11, 1947.

Svartbergm, Kenth. "Breed-Typical Behaviour in Dogs—Historical Remnants or Recent Constructs?" *Applied Animal Behaviour Science* 96, no. 3 (2006): 293–313.

Sidebar: Thinking About Risk

American Veterinary Medical Association. "US Pet Ownership Statistics." www.avma.org/KB/Resources/Statistics/Pages/Market-research -statistics-US-pet-ownership.aspx. Accessed April 16, 2016.

Bradley, Janis. *Dogs Bite, but Balloons and Slippers Are More Dangerous.* Berkeley, CA: James & Kenneth Publishers, 2005.

Gilchrist J., J. J. Sacks, D. White, and M. J. Kresnow. "Dog Bites: Still a Problem?" *Injury Prevention*, 14 (2008): 296–301.

National Canine Research Council. "Medically Attended Dog Bites." nationalcanineresearchcouncil.com/dogbites/medically-attended-dog-bites/. Accessed April 25, 2016.

——. "Reported Bites Decreasing." nationalcanineresearchcouncil.com/dogbites/reported-bites-decreasing/. Accessed April 25, 2016.

Chapter 3. How We See Pit Bulls Now

Brand, David. "Time Bombs on Legs: Violence-Prone Owners Are Turning Pit Bulls into Killers." *Time*, Monday, July 27, 1987.

"Brave bulldog Saves Twenty Women." *Washington Post*, July 31, 1907.

Colby, Joseph. *The American pit bull terrier*. Sacramento, CA: News Publishing Co., 1936.

Dickey, Bronwen. *Pit Bull: The Battle Over an American Icon*. New York: Alfred A. Knopf, 2016.

Healey, Mary. "Ban Pit Bulls." *Washington Post*, August 25, 1997.

Hearne, Vicki. *Bandit: Dossier of a Dangerous Dog*. New York: Harper Collins, 1991.

Sager, Mike. "A Boy and His Dog in Hell." *Rolling Stone*, July 2, 1987.

Shain, Stephanie. "Moving Beyond Breed." Presentation at Animal Care Expo, Humane Society of the United States, Nashville, TN, 2013.

Thurber, James. "A Snapshot of Rex." In *Thurber's Dogs*. New York: Simon and Schuster, 1955

Chapter 4. Pre-Owned Dogs

Blackwell, Emily J., Caroline Twells, Anne Seawright, and Rachel A. Casey. "The Relationship Between Training Methods and the Occurrence of Behavior Problems, as Reported by Owners, in a Population of Domestic Dogs." *Journal of Veterinary Behavior: Clinical Applications and Research* 3, (2008): 207–17.

Herron, Meghan E., Frances S. Shofer, and Ilana Reisner. "Survey of the Use and Outcome of Confrontational and Non-confrontational Training Methods in Client-Owned Dogs Showing Undesired Behaviors." *Applied Animal Behaviour Science* 117, (2009): 47–54.

Hiby E., N. Rooney, and J. Bradshaw. "Dog Training Methods: Their Use, Effectiveness and Interaction with Behaviour and Welfare." *Animal Welfare* 13 (2004): 63–69. dx.doi org/10.1016/j.jveb.2007.10.008.

Kwan, J. Y., and M. J. Bain. "Owner Attachment and Problem Behaviors Related to Relinquishment and Training Techniques of Dogs." *Journal of Applied Animal Welfare Science* 16 (2013): 168–83. doi: 10.1080/10888705.2013.768923.

Mondelli, F., E. Prato Previde, M. Verga, et al. "The Bond That Never Developed: Adoption and Relinquishment of Dogs in a Rescue Shelter." *Journal of Applied Animal Welfare Science* 7 (2004): 253-66.

New, John C. Jr., M. D. Salman, Mike King, Janet M. Scarlett, Philip H. Kass, and Jennifer M. Hutchison. "Characteristics of Shelter-Relinquished Animals and Their Owners Compared with Animals and Their Owners in U.S. Pet-Owning Households." *Journal of Applied Animal Welfare Science* 3 (2000). doi: 10.1207/S15327604JAWS0303_1.

Patronek, G. J., L. T. Glickman, A. M. Beck, G. P. McCabe, and C. Ecker. "Risk Factors for Relinquishment of Dogs to an Animal Shelter." *Journal of the American Veterinary Medicine Association* 209 (1996): 572–81.

Polsky, Richard. "Can Aggression in Dogs Be Elicited Through the Use of Electronic Pet Containment Systems?" *Journal of Applied Animal Welfare Science* 4 (2000): 345–57.

Schilder, M. B. H., and J. A. M. van der Borg. "Training Dogs with Help of the Shock Collar: Short and Long Term Behavioural Effects." *Applied Animal Behaviour Science* 85 (2004): 319–34.

Weiss, Emily, Margaret Slater, Laurie Garrison, Natasha Drain, Emily Dolan, Janet M. Scarlett, and Stephen L. Zawistowski. "Large Dog Relinquishment to Two Municipal Facilities in New York City and Washington, D.C.: Identifying Targets for Intervention." *Animals* 4 (2014): 409–33.

Chapter 5. Your Dog and the Law

"American Bar Association House of Delegates Resolution 100-2012." August 7, 2012. www.americanbar.org/content/dam/aba/administrative/mental _physical_disability/Resolution_100.authcheckdam.pdf.

"Ban and Outlaw Breed Specific Legislation (BSL) in the United States of America on a Federal Level!" Breed-Specific Legislation Is a Bad Idea." December 19, 2012. petitions.whitehouse.gov/petition/ ban-and-outlaw-breed-specific-legislation-bsl-united-states-america -federal-level-0. Accessed April 26, 2016.

BestFriendsVideos. "The Debate to End Breed Discrimination (BSL)." YouTube, 2014. www.youtube.com/watch?v=8yIkstRpCno. Accessed April 26, 2016.

"How to Avoid a Dog Bite." April 15, 2015. www.humanesociety.org/animals/ dogs/tips/avoid_dog_bites.html. Accessed April 26, 2016.

Huszai, Steven F. "Wooster Council Unanimously Agrees to Reverse Pit Bull Ban." *Daily Record*, April 16, 2013.

Klaassen, B., J. R. Buckley, and Aziz Esmail. "Does the Dangerous Dogs Act Protect Against Animal Attacks: A Prospective Study of Mammalian Bites in the Accident and Emergency Department." *Injury* 27, no. 2 (1996): 89–91. www.omaha-douglasconnection.com/images/ stories/38257DangerousDogs.pdf. Accessed October 2, 2008.

Madhani, Aamer. "U.S. Communities Increasingly Ditching Pit Bull Bans." *USA Today*. 2014. www.usatoday.com/story/news/nation/2014/11/17/pit -bulls-breed-specific-legislation-bans/19048719/. Accessed April 26, 2016.

Rosado, Belén, Sylvia García-Belenguer, Marta León, and Jorge Palacio. "Spanish Dangerous Animals Act: Effect on the Epidemiology of Dog Bites." *Journal of Veterinary Behavior: Clinical Applications and Research* 2, no. 5 (2007): 166–74. doi:10.1016/j.jveb.2007.07.010

Welsh, M. In *A Lawyer's Guide to Dangerous Dog Issues*, edited by Joan Schaffner. Chicago: Tort Trial & Insurance Practice Section, ABA, 2009, 39–46.

Additional resources referenced this chapter: StopBsl.org, BSLCensus .com, KC Dog Blog, Pinupsforpitbulls.org, PBLNN.com, nationalcanine researchcouncil.com.

Sidebar: The Dangers of Encouraging Any Breed-Specific Policy

"Animal Rights Uncompromised: 'Pets'" PETA. www.peta.org/about-peta /why-peta/pets/. Accessed April 26, 2016.

"What's the Kindest Thing We Can Do for Pit Bulls?" PETA Investigations. investigations.peta.org/breed-specific-protection. Accessed April 26, 2016.

Chapter 6. How to Talk to People About Pit Bulls

Sidebar: Myths About Pit Bulls

Erickson, Gregory M., Paul M. Gignac, Scott J. Steppan, A. Kristopher Lappin, Kent A. Vliet, John D. Brueggen, Brian D. Inouye, David Kledzik, and Grahame J. W. Webb. "Insights into the Ecology and Evolutionary Success of Crocodilians Revealed Through Bite-Force and Tooth-Pressure Experimentation." PLoS ONE 7(3): e31781. doi:10.1371/journal. pone.0031781, March 14, 2012.

Ellis, J. L., J. Thomason, E. Kebreab, K. Zubair, and J. France. "Cranial Dimensions and Forces of Biting in the Domestic Dog. *Journal of Anatomy*, 214 (2009): 362–73. doi: 10.1111/j.1469-7580.2008.01042.x.

"Interesting Account of Dogs." *Edinburgh Magazine: Or Literary Miscellany*, vol. 20. 1802.

Lindner, D. L., S. M. Marretta, G. J. Pijanowski, A. L. Johnson, and C. W. Smith. "Measurement of Bite Force in Dogs: A Pilot Study." *Journal of Veterinary Dentistry*, 12 (1995): 49–52.

online sources

Steffen Baldwin: www.actoh.org

Jane Berkey and Stacey Coleman www.animalfarmfoundation.org

Laura Chavarria: www.adoptwcac.org

Lili Chin: www.doggiedrawings.net/about

Brad Croft: Universal K9: www.universalk9inc.com

Karen Delise and Janis Bradley: nationalcanineresearchcouncil.com

Diane Jessup: workingpitbull.com

Angela Keith: www.meritpitbullfoundation.com

Ken Foster: www.nycacc.org

Sophie Gamand: www.sophiegamand.com

Heather Gutshall: www.handsomedansrescue.org

Lisa LaFontaine/Washington Humane Society–Washington Animal Rescue
    League: support.washhumane.org

Drayton Michaels: www.urbandawgs.com

Candice Miller: Roofus and Kilo: www.instagram.com/roofusandkilo

photo credits

acknowledgments

Much of this book could not have been written without relying on the hard work done by previous researchers and experts. In particular, we would like to thank Janis Bradley, Karen Delise, Bronwen Dickey, and Diane Jessup for being generous with their time and knowledge.

From Linda: I would especially like to thank everyone at Washington Humane Society–Washington Animal Rescue League for their help with this and many other projects, and for the many amazing photos that they allowed us to use.

From Deirdre: I would like to thank Leah Sauber for her incomparable assistance during the research phase of this book. I'd also like to thank my husband, Jeffrey, who has been amazing throughout the entire process of writing this book. My dogs, Zoe and Baxter Bean, for forgoing some snuggle time so that I could help write this book. I'd like to acknowledge Baxter Bean's efforts to thwart my writing by breaking my "O" key during the beginning phase of writing a book about dogs, where the "O" key is quite critical. My incredible volunteers, both nationally and internationally, who have helped to ensure that all dogs and their people receive equal treatment. I'd like to thank Linda Lombardi for co-authoring this book with me. It's been amazing to see what we could accomplish by teaming up. I hope that we get to do more together! Dan Crissman, our amazing editor, for believing in our work and for helping to further this cause for dogs like Charlie and Carla Lou. Thanks to our literary agent, Jim McCarthy, and to everyone who submitted artwork and photographs, and, most of all, to those of you who took the time to be interviewed. We're all in this together! —xo Deirdre 'Little Darling' Franklin

Deirdre Franklin: pinupsforpitbulls.org
Linda Lombardi: www.lindalombardi.com

index

Animal Care and Control (ACC), 175
animal cruelty cases, 191
    See also dogfighting
Animal Cruelty Task Force of Ohio (ACT
        Ohio), 189–90
Animal Farm Foundation (AFF), 75–81,
        213
animal shelters. *See* shelters
anxiety and fear issues, 108, 109, 111–15,
        126–27
Applied Animal Behaviour Science, 51
attacks
    fatalities, 50
    German shepherds, 42, 45–47
    media coverage of, 49–50
    protecting against, 145
    See also aggression; dog bites
Australian cattle dogs, 51

B

bait dog myth, 72–73
Baldwin, Steffen, 185–94
beagles, 51
behavioral issues
    with shelter surrenders, 92–94
    stress signals, 111–13
    See also pre-owned dogs, public behavior
        of; training methods
behavior traits, breed-specific, 54–56
    See also aggression
Belgian Malinois, 197
Berkey, Jane, 75, 213
bite pressure, 169, 197
bites. *See* dog bites
bloodhounds, 36–41, 130
border collies, 24, 55

breed bans. *See* breed-specific legislation
        (BSL)
breed identification
    breed characteristics, 104–8
    DNA studies for, 27–33
    past traditions, 17, 19
    purebred breeds, 20–23
    in shelters, 23, 25–26
breed neutrality
    enacting laws on, 142–43
    as shelter policy, 84–88
    See also breed-specific legislation
        (BSL)
breed reputations, 35–61
    behavior traits, 54–57, 59
    changing through history, 36–41
    dog attacks, 49–50
    dog bite statistics, 47–50, 58–59
    genetics and environment, 59–61
    good *vs.* bad stereotypes, 42–47
    scientific studies, 51–55
    See also pit bull image
breed-specific legislation (BSL), 129–55
    about, 130
    adverse effects of, 148
    American Bar Association Position
        Statement on, 152
    bans enacted and lifted, 135–38
    children affected by, 150
    city and county legislation (US),
        133–35
    community advocates against, 155
    European legislation, 54, 131–33
    fighting back against, 142–47
    housing issues and, 154–55
    PETA policies and, 153

environment, genes and, 59–61

euthanization, 73–75, 82–89

F

family *vs.* resident dogs, defined, 147

fear and anxiety issues, 108, 109, 111–15,
  126–27

fierceness in pit bulls, 64–65

Florida legislation, 137

Foster, Ken, 173–78

fostering and rescuing dogs, 99–101, 198–206

Frank, Morris, 43–44

G

Gamand, Sophie, 178–85

genetic factors
  aggression and, 57, 59
  and environment, 59–61
  See also breed identification

German shepherds, 35–36, 42–47, 51,
  131–32, 169

growling, 113, 127

guide dogs, 43–44

Gutshall, Heather, 106–8, 109

H

Hearne, Vicki, 14, 73

historical views. *See* breed reputations; pit
  bull image

housing issues, 154–55

humane law enforcement, 187–92

I

image of pit bulls. *See* pit bull image

Indianapolis (IN), advocacy in, 207–13

insurance issues, 150–52

Italy legislation, 132

J

Jack Russell terriers, 51

Jessup, Diane, 14, 15, 16, 24, 57

Journal of Veterinary Behavior, 131–32

K

Keith, Angela, 94–96, 101, 109

L

Labrador retrievers, 23, 24, 56, 116, 135,
  198, 200, 203, 213

LaFontaine, Lisa, 82–89

law enforcement, humane, 187–92

A Lawyer's Guide to Dangerous Dog Issues,
  144–45

legal challenges. *See* breed-specific legislation (BSL)

Little Darling's Pinups for Pitbulls (Franklin),
  73–74

M

media sources
  communicating with, 165, 166–67
  coverage of dog attacks, 49–50
  promoting sensationalism, 71–73

Merit Pit Bull Foundation, 94

Michaels, Drayton, 111–19

Miller, Candice, 198–206

mixed-breed dogs, 27–33

Monadnock Humane Society, 83

Moreauville (LA) ban, 136

myths and legends, 108–10, 169

N

National Canine Research Council (NCRC),
  36, 147

The Netherlands legislation, 131